First published 1993

ISBN 0 7110 2078 7

© Mike Esau & Gerald Siviour, 1993

Published by Ian Allan Ltd, Shepperton, Surrey; and printed by Ian Allan Printing Ltd at their works at Coombelands in Runnymede, England.

*Front cover top:*
**In 1948 an all-Pullman train, the summer only 'Thanet Belle' returned to the Ramsgate line for the first time in over 20 years. It is seen here in charge of 'Battle of Britain' Pacific No S21C157 *Biggin Hill.*** *E. R. Wethersett*

*Front cover, bottom:*
**A Continental express of the 1930s leaves Dover Marine for Victoria headed by 'Lord Nelson' No 854 *Howard of Effingham,* a type built with the needs of the boat trains in mind.** *By courtesy of the National Railway Museum, York*

*Rear cover top:*
**By the 1950s, Maunsell corridor coaches were much in evidence on local trains. In this view a three coach set and other assorted vehicles form a train from Maidstone East to Margate leaving Broadstairs behind 'D' class No 31574.** *Revd A. W. V. Mace*

*Rear cover, centre:*
**Early summer on the Kent coast in the mid 1950s with 'Schools' No 30914 *Eastbourne* climbing the 1 in 93 out of Herne Bay with the 11.35am Victoria to Ramsgate train on Saturday 19 May 1956.** *J. J. Smith*

*Rear cover, bottom:*
**Shortly before it was rebuilt, 'Merchant Navy' Pacific No 35001 *Channel Packet* paid a return visit to the Dover line. In rather grubby condition the locomotive is seen passing Beckenham Junction in August 1958.** *P. J. Lynch*

*Previous page:*
**Dover regularly handled VIP trains carrying presidents and royalty to and from London. This scene, taken on 7 March 1950, shows a special conveying President Auriol of France to London approaching Shakespeare Cliff tunnel. The engine 'Merchant Navy' No 35019 *French Line CGT* brought from Nine Elms to the Eastern Section for the occasion.** *P. Ransome Wallis collection, National Railway Museum, York*

# Contents

Preface     5

Chapter 1     7
**Introduction - the evolution of Kent's main lines**

Chapter 2     15
**The main lines described**

Chapter 3     34
**Principal junctions and traffic centres**

Chapter 4     48
**The Continental expresses**

Chapter 5     58
**The Kent coast expresses**

Chapter 6     69
**Summer weekends**

Chapter 7     78
**The Hoppers Specials**

Chapter 8     83
**Stopping trains**

Chapter 9     90
**Freight traffic**

Chapter 10     98
**Out of the ordinary**

Chapter 11     105
**The decline and revival of steam**

Appendix     112

Bibliography     112

# Acknowledgements

The authors wish to record their grateful thanks to the following:
Mrs Diana Siviour, who typed the manuscript.
Mr Peter Landon for help with the fieldwork and for checking the manuscript.
Mr Bernard Haste and the staff of Ashford Borough Library whose Railway Room provided excellent research facilities.
Mr Mike Cutland, Mr Mike Bunn, Dr Ralph Tutton and other members of the 'Talking of Trains' class at Surbiton for help with ideas and research.
Mr Vic Mitchell of Middleton Press for permission to quote from *War on the Line* by B. Darwin.

# KENT COAST
# HEYDAY

## MIKE ESAU & GERALD SIVIOUR

IAN ALLAN Publishing

# KENT COAST HEYDAY

# Preface

Compared to the ordered routes of the Southern's Western Section, which progressively branched out from Waterloo, the lines to Kent wove a complex pattern. This was reflected in the varied train services, and the astonishing range of locomotives that could be seen working them in the 1950s.

My youthful introduction to the Kent coast lines was inevitably through train spotting trips to London Bridge or Victoria. A wonderful view of the busy service at Victoria could be enjoyed from the end of a long platform on the 'Brighton' side, and it is memories of those days which probably gave me the idea for this book. In the years immediately after World War 2 there were striking differences in the locomotives operating the passenger services, for aged Drummond 'T9' 4-4-0s were still at work on summer Saturday expresses alongside new Bulleid Pacifics — to be near a 'West Country' at Victoria mightily blowing off steam from a boiler pressed to 280lb/sq in, was an aural experience not easily forgotten!

Time at Victoria was sometimes followed up with a visit to Stewarts Lane depot across the river, whose yard, crowded with smoking engines waiting to back down to the terminus, contrasted with the silent extremities of the roads inside the shed. Here elderly engines slumbered in the gloom disturbed only by the occasional rumble of trains passing overhead on the South London line, and the fluttering of pigeons which nested in the sooty roof.

One of the oddities of the Eastern Division engines was the haphazard positioning of classes within the '31000' series numbering sequence, so until 'U' class No 31610 was reached, and order restored, only the well versed could remember which number belonged to which class. Scattered among these numbers were the survivors of the elegant 'D' and 'E' classes from the Wainwright express locomotive era, as well as the charming and useful 'H' class tank engines, and the ancient looking 'O1' 0-6-0s which worked the Headcorn to Rolvenden section of the Emmett-like Kent and East Sussex Railway. Of the bigger engines, the Kent lines were also home to most of the later series of the 'King Arthurs' in the 1950s, and who can forget the evocative names of such knights as Nos 30797 *Sir Blamor de Ganis*, 30799 *Sir Ironside*, and of course the incomparable 30803 *Sir Harry le Fise Lake*.

In order to see something of this marvellous assortment of locomotives, I enjoyed several journeys to Kent railway centres such as Ashford and Tonbridge. A typical visit was made on Tuesday 27 April 1954, a day of long sunny spells and only a little light cloud. Looking back nearly 40 years, the details from my notebook make fascinating reading.

With a friend I travelled up to Waterloo from my home at Malden, passing the 9.54am train to Basingstoke which was hauled as usual by one of the clumpy Urie 'H15s' No 30486, whilst No 35017 *Belgian Marine* was waiting to work the down 11am 'Atlantic Coast Express'. Crossing over to Waterloo East we caught the 11.15am train from Charing Cross, and were able to savour the journey in a large windowed Bulleid saloon coach until the 12.39pm arrival at Ashford. This service was hauled by 'Battle of Britain' No 34085, later *501 Squadron*, for it had no nameplate at this time.

The short walk round to the works entrance from the station never failed to generate a sense of expectation, culminating in arrival at the gatehouse with its distinctive clocktower. Promptly at 1.30pm we were allowed into the works and hurried to the scrapyard adjacent to the main line, for normally only tantalisingly brief glimpses of this area could be seen from passing trains. Here we found one of the last two 'E' class 4-4-0s, No 31315 still with 'BRITISH RAILWAYS' in shaded lettering on its tender. This engine had arrived from Redhill a few weeks earlier, where it had occasionally been used on the steeply graded line to Guildford, in between lengthy periods in store. In company with No 31315, was the last surviving Southern engine not renumbered into the '30000' series, 'D' class No s1493. The 'D' had spent a number of years rusting away in the salty air at St Leonards shed, almost forgotten at the end of an outlying siding. Still displaying stately lines despite loss of its tender, was 'T9' No 30282 from Eastleigh shed, a sad reminder of the time when the class worked on the Thanet lines. Thirty-eight engines were at the works, and in contrast to the condition of No s1493, it was heartening to see a 'D' class No 31577 being overhauled, though this was likely to be its last. One of the rare Exmouth Junction 'N' class was up for a general repair, together with no less than six 'U1' three-cylinder 2-6-0s, possibly being attended to before the intensive summer passenger service started.

A short walk along Newtown Road and across the small level crossing over the main line, brought us to the concrete built shed where thirty-eight engines were seen, including one or two fresh from the works, such as 'E4' No 32487 based at Guildford. Motive power modernisation in the form of the BR 'Standard' classes had yet to make any impact on sheds such as Ashford, and so many pre-grouping veterans were present, such as 'D' class No 31574, used on local passenger services.

Returning to the station, 'Schools' class No 30935 *Sevenoaks* took us back to Tonbridge where the shed was visited at 5.15pm. Twenty-four engines were seen, and in common with Ashford, it was characteristic of the time that about three-quarters of these were of pre-grouping origin — few other parts of the country could offer such a venerable collection of motive power in the mid 1950s. Of note was the last operational 'E' 4-4-0 No 31166, which usually worked services to Eastbourne and Brighton, an 'R' and two 'R1' 0-4-4Ts, out of use at the limits of the shed yard, and several 'C' class 0-6-0s, whose solid and conventional design contrasted with their modern 'Q1' class counterparts. The locomotives seen at Ashford and Tonbridge are listed in the Appendix.

Rather than going direct to Charing Cross, it was far more interesting to come home via the old main line through Redhill. So it was that we travelled into the westering sun on the 5.45pm SX train from Tonbridge to Edenbridge, a 'rush hour' service utilising a spare push and pull set. This was hauled tender first by 'D1' class No 31489, which, after arrival at 6.03pm, returned the coaches empty to Tonbridge.

After a short wait in the evening light on the staggered platform which overlooked the town, 'H' class No 31552 came bustling into the station with the Redhill train, amid a cloud of smoke. Apart from the short section by electric train from Redhill to Croydon, steam haulage could be enjoyed all the way to Clapham Junction by picking up an Oxted line train at East Croydon, on this occasion in charge of 4MT 2-6-4T No 42104.

Such was a typical journey towards the end of the heyday years of Kent coast steam, when trains as different in character as the prestigious all Pullman 'Golden Arrow', and humble hop pickers' specials, composed of the most expendable in rolling stock and motive power, ran through scenery which ranged from reedy coastal marshes to rounded chalk downland. The story of this heyday, and the relationship of the train services to the towns, industries and environment of the region, is an absorbing one, which Gerald Siviour so ably reveals in the chapters which follow.

*Mike Esau*
July 1992

*Frontispiece*
**The postwar heyday years of the 1950s briefly lived again at London
Bridge just before midnight on Sunday 7 June 1992, when former
Ramsgate Pacific No 34027** *Taw Valley* **arrived hauling the first steam
hauled express passenger train on the main line from Ashford for over
30 years. The engine and stock were returning from an event marking
the 150th anniversary of railways at Ashford.** *Mike Esau*

# Chapter 1

# Introduction- the evolution of Kent's main lines

Some of the events that affected the evolution of Kent's main line railway network took place far back in geological time. The most recent was, perhaps, the most important. This was the rise in sea level which took place at the end of the great ice age, when large quantities of water released from glaciers caused coastal flooding on a world wide scale. In south east England this resulted in the creation, some eight to nine thousand years ago, of the Straits of Dover, giving Britain its status as an island. The cliffs of France are still a familiar sight from Folkestone and Dover, but both the English and continental coasts draw rapidly away from this point of approach and their mutual visibility is soon lost.

Places on either side of this strip of water, just over 20 miles wide, have naturally become the focal point of routeways between Britain and the continent, Kent becoming the gateway to England despite a lack of good natural harbours. Whereas in other parts of the country the need to provide transport for minerals, especially coal, encouraged railway construction, in Kent it was the need to speed the transit of mail and passengers to Dover that was the main stimulus to the building of the South Eastern Railway's route from Redhill, the county's first main line. Subsequently the London, Chatham and Dover Railway provided an alternative route and intense competition between the companies before their eventual amalgamation in 1899 led to the building of

a dense network of lines, some of which (like those to Port Victoria and Dungeness) originated as attempts to provide access to alternative port facilities (Fig 1).

On the journey between London and the Kent coast, the gradient profiles of these main lines are profoundly influenced by the geology and landforms of the county. Particularly important are the Chalk ridge of the North Downs and the uplands formed by the Lower Greensand, both running in a broadly west to east direction through the county and reaching heights in excess of 600ft (Fig 2). Both have steep escarpments facing south and more gentle dip-slopes northwards towards London and the Thames estuary. The SER main line between Tonbridge and the outskirts of London best illustrates the influence of these ridges. North of Tonbridge it climbs steeply to pierce the crest of the Greensand ridge in Sevenoaks Tunnel, while from Dunton Green it climbs again (Fig 3) to cut through the highest part of the Chalk in Polhill Tunnel. East of Tonbridge the line makes use of the extensive lowland eroded in the soft Weald Clay of the Vale of Kent to reach Ashford. To the south lies another belt of sandy upland country, through which runs the SER line to Hastings and into which branch lines like that to Hawkhurst threaded their way.

The rocks of the Weald were originally laid down under the sea or in lakes and deltas during Cretaceous times, some 150

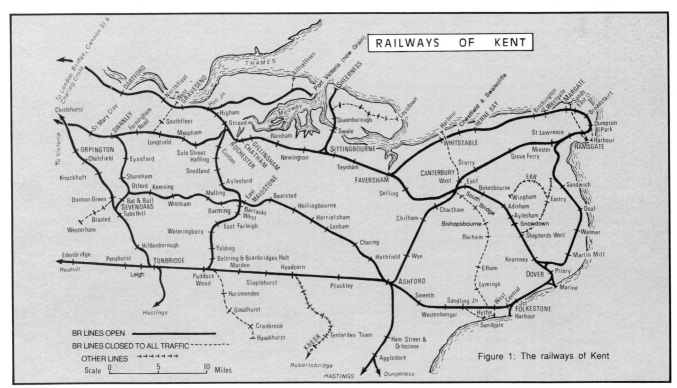

Figure 1: The railways of Kent

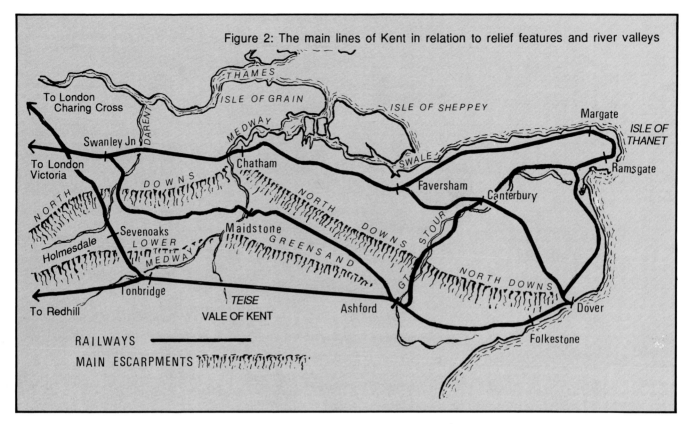

Figure 2: The main lines of Kent in relation to relief features and river valleys

RAILWAYS ━━━━━━━

MAIN ESCARPMENTS ⁓⁓⁓⁓⁓⁓⁓

million years ago, the Chalk being a white limestone made partly of fossils and partly of plant remains. Following their formation southern England was, around 35 million years ago, subjected to the great period of earth movements which further south in Europe formed the high mountain ranges of the Alps, the Pyrenees and the Carpathians. The present Weald came to be occupied by a dome-shaped upland, several thousands of feet high. Upon it the forces of erosion began to work, the rivers etching out lowlands where soft rocks like the Weald clay were exposed near the crest of the ridge. Thus the Vale of Kent, which became such an important feature to the nineteenth century railway builders, was created. Elsewhere the more resistant Chalk and sandstones remained upstanding as ridges (Fig 2).

The northern and southern margins of the Wealden dome continued to be trimmed by the sea, which gradually retreated northwards towards the Thames basin and southwards towards the English Channel. As it did so a number of northward flowing rivers, notably the Darent, Medway and Stour came into

*Right:*
**The evolution of the Kent Coast main line network began at Redhill, with the building, from a junction with the Brighton line, of the SER's original main line to Dover, opened in stages in the early 1840s. When the direct route from London to Tonbridge via Orpington was completed in 1868, the Redhill to Tonbridge section became something of a backwater. Towards the end of the steam age the most important passenger train to use it was the weekday express from Birkenhead to the south via Reading. The Kent coast portion is seen leaving Redhill in August 1960 behind 'Schools' No 30927** *Clifton. Gerald Siviour*

8

existence, cutting the prominent gaps through the North Downs which are such a striking feature of the area today (Fig 2). These gaps are used as routeways by secondary lines, but to the LCDR main line they presented obstacles to be crossed in its journey across the North Downs dip-slope, accounting in part for the switchback nature of the route (Fig 4). Westbound trains in particular are confronted with a formidable five mile climb, mainly at 1 in 100, out of the Medway gap to Sole Street station.

In the words of Kidner ( *The South Eastern & Chatham Railway, 1952* ) 'railways entered Kent by the side door', the original main line to Dover being a branch from the London-Brighton line at Redhill (known as Reigate until 1858). The route between Redhill and Norwood was built by the LBSCR, but the SER had running powers over it and purchased the Coulsdon to Redhill section in 1842. It made use of the pass known as the Merstham wind-gap, through which the upper part of the River

*Above:*
**The view westward from Tonbridge station, showing the junction between the Redhill line on the left and the London line curving away to the right, with the west goods yard between them. The curve has been eased several times and work is seen in progress on Sunday 27 April 1958 with 'C' class 0-6-0s Nos 31219 and 31585 in attendance. As this book went to press the curve was again being realigned to raise the speed limit for the forthcoming Channel Tunnel expresses.**
*B. Fletcher*

*Below:*
**The direct route from Tonbridge to London brings trains into conflict with the physical geography of the Weald due to the need to cross the ridges of the Lower Greensand and the North Downs. In April 1958 'H' class No 31193 is seen propelling two rail motor coaches bound for duty on the Westerham branch up the 1 in 122 past Weald box to Sevenoaks tunnel, by which the line cuts through the Greensand ridge dominating the skyline.** *Mike Esau*

*Above:*
**By contrast the main line east of Tonbridge runs straight and almost level along the lowland eroded in the clay of the central Weald. This view eastward from Paddock Wood shows a local train headed by 'Q1' class No 33028 arriving from the Maidstone West branch. The bay used by Hawkhurst trains is on the right, whilst 'H' class No 31308 shunts stock in the siding beyond.** *Mike Esau*

*Below:*
**Folkestone Junction, the town's first permanent station, was opened in December 1843. This view looking eastward towards Martello tunnel shows the staggered platforms characteristic of SER stations, and the sidings on the right where the boat trains reverse for the journey down to the harbour. 'D1' class No 31739 is seen calling with the 7.24am London Bridge to Ramsgate train in the last days of steam on the Kent main lines. The station was renamed Folkestone East in 1962 and closed to the public three years later.** *Mike Esau*

Wandle may once have flowed, to provide a route across the barrier of the North Downs. The line opened in stages to Ashford on 1 December 1842 and to Folkestone in June 1843. At first a temporary terminal on the site of the present Central station was used and passengers had to walk or use horse-drawn carriages to reach Telford's original Folkestone harbour. Despite the problems of crossing the deep Foord Valley and negotiating the unstable cliff section to the east, the first passenger train ran to Dover in February 1844. During the rest of the 1840s and immediately afterwards a number of branches were constructed from the Redhill-Dover spine (Fig 1), so that by the early 1850s the SER had a route mileage of 267, and much of central, south and east Kent was within reach of a railway.

North Kent, by contrast, was relatively badly served, a situation only partly compensated for by the use of stage coaches

on Watling Street and water transport on the lower Thames and its tributaries. Rail connection with the Medway Towns was first made from Gravesend to Strood by laying rails along the towpath of the Thames and Medway Canal. In 1846 this was purchased by the SER, following which it was drained and rails laid in part along its bed, a service between Denton (for Gravesend) and Strood restarting in August 1847. In the early 1850s the newly formed East Kent Railway obtained powers to continue the line from Strood eastwards to Canterbury and subsequently to Dover to provide access (for the towns of northern and interior Kent) to the short sea route. Faversham was reached in 1858, Canterbury in 1860 (by which time the company was known as the London, Chatham and Dover Railway) and Dover itself in 1861, seventeen years later than the SER. At first temporary terminals were used, but from 1864 'Chatham' line boat trains joined SER trains in using the bleak and windswept station on the Admiralty Pier. Betting on which company's train from London would arrive first became a popular pastime in Dover.

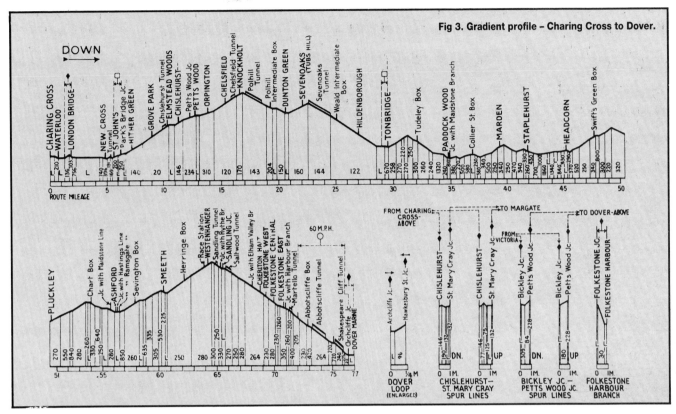

Fig 3. Gradient profile – Charing Cross to Dover.

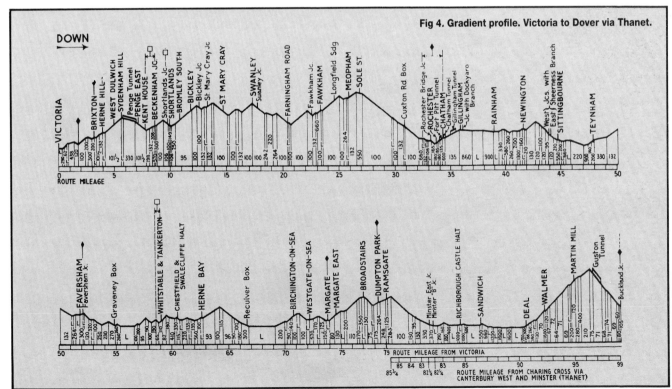

Fig 4. Gradient profile. Victoria to Dover via Thanet.

Intense competition between the rival companies led both to seek shorter routes to Dover. The SER completed its cut-off route from south east London to Tonbridge in 1868, shortening the distance by thirteen miles compared with the original route via Redhill. Meanwhile the LCDR, originating some 30 miles from London and with an easy route to it blocked by the SER lines in North Kent, was forced to take a difficult route across the Chalk uplands towards Swanley and Bromley. The first stage was to build its own extension from Rochester to St Mary Cray. From here to Bromley it ran over the eastern extension of the Mid Kent Railway, while from Bromley (Shortlands) to Beckenham Junction it used the track of the West End of London and Crystal Palace Railway's extension to reach Balham, Clapham Junction and Battersea. In 1860 the LBSCR leased the Victoria and Pimlico Railway, which was also used by the LCDR to gain a foothold north of the Thames close to fashionable Belgravia. From 1 November 1861 the LCDR began exercising its running powers over this odd collection of suburban railways to give it a line to Dover nearly 10 miles shorter than its older rival. So began in earnest the bitter feud between them that was to last for nearly 40 years.

*Above:*

**The main purpose of building Kent's first main lines was to reach the port of Dover to make connection with the packet steamers to France. Over a century later, in the heyday years of the all-Pullman 'Golden Arrow', unrebuilt 'Merchant Navy' No 35028** *Clan Line* **runs beneath the Western Heights at the approach to Dover Marine on 17 June 1951.** *Les Elsey*

A final stage in the evolution of routes to Dover took place some years later, when the LCDR built a branch from Otford, on the Swanley-Sevenoaks line, to Maidstone East (opened in 1874) and subsequently extended it along the Vale of Holmesdale to Ashford in 1884. Originally the LCDR had their

*Below:*

**In its journey from London to the coast the LCDR main line experiences several undulations as its cuts across the valleys of the rivers draining northwards towards the Thames estuary. The major river gap in the North Downs is that of the Medway, seen in the background of this view of an up express, headed by 'King Arthur' No 30769** *Sir Balan*, **beginning the five mile climb, mainly at 1 in 100, to Sole Street on Easter Monday 11 April 1955.** *S. C. Nash*

*Above:*
**Because of the need to cross deep river valleys, the LCDR main line has several notable viaducts, especially at St Mary Cray and Farningham Road. Less spectacular but no less graceful is the one at Eynsford, by which the line from Swanley to Sevenoaks and Maidstone East spans the Darent valley. A 'C' class 0-6-0 is seen crossing with a goods in the 1930s.** *Revd A. W. V. Mace*

own station known as Ashford West, but its use was short lived and all trains used the SER station from 1 January 1899. Although like many other lines in Kent it was born mainly out of rivalry between the two companies and personal antagonism between their chairmen (Sir Edward Watkin of the SER and

*Below:*
**The last of the main routes to the Kent coast to be completed was the LCDR line from Maidstone East to Ashford. Electrification from London reached Maidstone in 1939 and for over 20 years it was the frontier between the electric trains seen on the far left and the steam locals from Ashford. On the down line 'Q1' class No 33033 heads a local goods in the Ashford direction on Saturday 15 April 1961.** *J. J. Smith*

James Forbes of the 'Chatham'), the Maidstone East line became a very useful extra link to the coast. At times of heavy continental, holiday and hop-pickers' traffic it provided relief for the principal main lines and today remains valuable as a diversionary route when engineering works close the main line via Tonbridge.

Although the provision of links to the ferry or packet ports was the main incentive to railway construction in Kent it was not the only one, for the county was important for its seaside resorts long before the coming of the railways. Margate was a port which attracted large numbers of visitors who came from London by the Thames steam boats, while Ramsgate was a more up-market resort which enjoyed the patronage of the nobility and still retains fine examples of Georgian architecture. Both were reached by the SER from Ashford via Canterbury in 1846. It was a somewhat roundabout journey from London, especially to Margate, which was usually reached after reversal at Ramsgate Town station (Fig 5). More direct communication with the capital was established in 1863 with the opening of the LCDR's route from Faversham across the marshes through Whitstable to Herne Bay and on to Margate, Broadstairs and Ramsgate Harbour. Both Ramsgate terminals were cramped and operationally diffi-

*Above:*
**The junction at Faversham between the original LCDR main line to Dover and the later direct line to the Thanet resorts curving away to the left. On the last Saturday of steam working, 13 June 1959, 'L1' class 4-4-0 No 31754 heads the 4.52pm Chatham to Ramsgate train, while steam remains much in evidence at the engine shed. This remained in use for several years as a diesel depot and a part survives today.** *R. C. Riley*

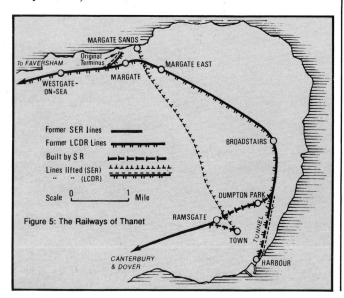

Figure 5: The Railways of Thanet

cult and were replaced in 1926 with a new through station as part of a rationalisation of railways in Thanet (Fig 5).

Although many features of the economy of Kent pre-date the railways there is no doubt that improved transport did much to stimulate further development. More resorts appeared while a new coalfield was opened up, providing some of the raw materials for industrial growth. Agriculture benefited from improved access to markets and the increased availability of the casual labour upon which hop growing in particular depended, while early in the 20th century the coastal strip around Whitstable and Herne Bay established a trend by becoming one of the first centres of long-distance commuting to London.

In the heyday years of Kentish steam between the late 1920s and the early 1960s passenger traffic was handled by locomotives ranging latterly from Bulleid's 'Merchant Navy' class and light Pacifics to a range of types designed by Richard Maunsell mainly in Southern Railway days. Freight and local services employed many veterans which had originated on the SECR and its constituents. The range of passenger coaches was equally varied, from the elegant Pullmans of the 'Golden Arrow' and the blue Wagons-Lits vehicles of the 'Night Ferry' to wooden bodied non-corridors of SECR origin, with their distinctive 'birdcage' guard's lookout. To the vast range of freight vehicles seen everywhere in those days was added the dimension of many continental wagons which had arrived by train ferry. It all provided a richly varied railway scene to set against the backcloth of the attractive countryside of the Garden of England and it is the atmosphere of this vanished steam railway system that this book aims to recapture.

# Chapter 2

# The main lines described

1. **Charing Cross to Dover**
2. **Victoria to Dover**
3. **The coastal route — Faversham to Dover via Thanet**

## 1. Charing Cross to Dover.

The South Eastern Railway's West End terminus, opened in 1864 on the site of Hungerford Market, is the most centrally situated of all the capital's main line stations, for in its forecourt stands the somewhat anonymous Eleanor Cross, to which all signpost and milepost distances to London are measured. Situated close to theatreland and within easy walk of some of the smartest hotels and restaurants the station front still presents an impressive façade despite being surrounded today by modern glass and concrete buildings. The frontage is dominated by the tall windows and balconies of the 250 bedroom hotel, opened in 1865 to be worthy of the international travellers for whom it was provided. Behind it the station is of only modest proportions with six platforms, numbers five and six being those generally used for Hastings and Kent coast trains. The station once had an all-over arched roof. When this collapsed in 1905 it was replaced by a much flatter one above which recent building has taken place.

The traveller from Charing Cross faces one of the slowest exits from any London terminus, for even main line trains may make two stops, at Waterloo East and London Bridge, in the first two miles of their journey. They have also to negotiate a tortuous route over one of Britain's busiest junctions at Borough Market, where the lines from Cannon Street join, so that even today's electric expresses are allowed seven minutes from Charing Cross to leaving London Bridge. In steam days the allowance was up to 11 minutes, but the fastest trains were allowed only six and a half minutes to pass London Bridge. However, compensation is provided by views from the train that are always interesting and sometimes splendid, especially in the light of a stormy evening, for the entire line out to New Cross is at high level over arches, in contrast to the tunnels and cuttings of the northern routes from the capital.

A fine vista of Westminster opens out to the south as soon as the train rumbles out of Charing Cross on to Hungerford Bridge. The tree-lined Embankment along which, until July 1952, London's last tram route ran, leads towards Westminster Bridge and the Houses of Parliament and Big Ben, with the former County Hall on the opposite side of the river. To the north is the skyline of the City of London, dominated by the dome of St Paul's until the office building boom of the last 30 years swamped the site of medieval London.

*Below:*
**A view of Charing Cross in 1959, showing the squat flat roof which replaced the original all-over arch following its collapse in 1905. Kent coast and Hastings trains normally use platforms 5 and 6 on the left but this photograph was probably taken during the rush hour period when main line trains departed from Cannon Street. The four coach EPB electric units were still operating on the Kent suburban lines over 30 years later.** *R. C. Riley*

All trains call at one of the four platforms, lettered A to D to avoid confusion with the main station, of Waterloo East. This was known until 1935 as Waterloo Junction, and it is still possible to discern, on the right hand side before reaching the station, the site of a little-used spur which once connected to the LSWR terminus. Beyond Waterloo East the main line is crossed by the LCDR route from Herne Hill to the City. This mainly served the needs of suburban traffic bound for Blackfriars and Holborn Viaduct and today is of increasing importance as part of the Thameslink network. Until the 1960s around 40 freight trains a day passed through the Holborn Viaduct Low Level tunnel to reach the Great Northern and Midland lines. Both the spur climbing from Metropolitan Junction, on the SE line, and the Herne Hill line, were therefore constantly busy with the passage of mixed freight trains, usually pulled by LMS Jinties or 2-6-2T or LNER 'N1', 'J50' or 'J52' tanks bound from Hither Green to the northern yards. Southwark goods depot, built for continental traffic, and Ewer Street locomotive servicing point were also located nearby.

As the main line curves past Southwark Cathedral towards Borough Market Junction there is a view down into the market, one of London's oldest, but one which remains busy despite the competition of the new Covent Garden Market further south on the site of Nine Elms engine shed. London Bridge is both London's oldest main line terminus and one of its most interesting. It began life in 1836 as the western terminus of the London and Greenwich Railway; by the early 1840s its use was shared by the SER and the LBSCR who, in order to avoid high tolls charged by the Greenwich company, forsook the use of London Bridge in 1844 for their own terminus at Bricklayer's Arms in the Old Kent Road. Passengers failed to share the view of the railway companies that this constituted a 'grand West End terminus'. The Greenwich Railway also reduced its tolls so that by 1852 Bricklayer's Arms had ceased to handle regular passenger

*Above:*
**A view of the route out of Charing Cross over Hungerford Bridge taken from the roof of Waterloo station on 2 October 1946. A new 'West Country' Pacific No 21C132 (later named *Camelford*) is seen heading a down Kent coast express. The Royal Festival Hall (to the right of the railway) and the Shell Centre (to the left), now occupy the site of the war battered buildings seen in the picture.** *By courtesy of the National Railway Museum, York*

*Below:*
**Many London terminals had sidings nearby where steam engines could be turned and serviced without returning to the main shed. Those reaching Charing Cross used the facilities at Ewer Street close to Metropolitan Junction. 'Schools' No 901 *Winchester* is seen at Ewer Street in the 1940s with some of its cab windows blanked out as a wartime protection measure.** *S. C. Townroe*

*Right:*
**A cross London freight from the Great Northern section emerges from Snow Hill tunnel beneath the now vanished Holborn Viaduct station on Wednesday 4 August 1954. The engine is 'J50' class 0-6-0T No 68928. Holborn Viaduct was the LCDR City of London terminus and was once served by Continental expresses. Towards the end it handled mainly commuter and vans trains, and in this picture one of the latter is being shunted by 'C' class No 31723.** *R. C. Riley*

*Centre right:*
**The volume of traffic over Borough Market Junction, whose signalbox can be seen to the right of Southwark Cathedral, is apparent in this rush hour picture taken in the 1950s. The steam train is one of the evening commuter services from Cannon Street to the Chatham line, headed by Faversham 'D1' No 31494. In the bottom right hand corner is the spur to Metropolitan Junction, with the main line from Charing Cross forming the third side of the triangle out of sight behind the buildings of Borough Market.**
*R. C. Riley*

*Bottom right:*
**London Bridge is the capital's oldest main line station. The former LBSCR terminus is out of sight to the left of this picture which features the SER low level platforms and the high level lines heading for Charing Cross and Cannon Street. 'D1' No 31735 is seen departing with a vans train on Thursday 14 May 1959. In those days the City skyline was dominated by the dome of St Paul's Cathedral and the cranes of the Pool of London and the other up-river docks.** *R. C. Riley*

trains, although a great goods depot on the site functioned for a further 130 years. Passenger operations moved back to London Bridge, where first a joint station and then separate terminals were opened for the SER in 1851 and the LBSCR in 1854. Part of the façade of the former disappeared when the Charing Cross and Cannon Street high level extension opened in the late 1860s. Apart from the removal of No 5 through road in 1952 the layout of the High Level station remained the same from the 1890s, when an additional platform and the SER offices at 84 Tooley Street were built on the north side, until rebuilding took place in the 1970s. This was followed in the early 1990s by further alterations to accommodate future Thameslink traffic.

For the next three miles towards New Cross the Dover line crosses the widened London and Greenwich Railway arches, built over the alluvium of the River Thames terraces. Although they added greatly to the cost of both the original line and its subsequent widening, the arches became a great landscape feature in this flat area south of the river and were likened at the time of their construction to a Roman Aqueduct. From them there is a view northwards towards Tower Bridge and the City skyline, while on each side of the railway is a mixture of modern flats and the tightly packed streets of that part of London's inner nineteenth century suburbs that survived the blitz and postwar slum clearance schemes. These inner boroughs were the capital's industrial heartland before congestion and space limitations caused many firms to move to locations nearer the fringe of the urban area, leaving behind much wasteland. Southwark and Bermondsey were particularly associated with the food, brewing, distilling and printing trades, examples of all of which can still be seen. The district further south is a hilly one and the skyline is dominated by the gravel-capped London Clay ridges rising towards Beulah Hill and Upper Norwood. The mast at Crystal Palace is a prominent feature, the land rising to over 400ft.

South of New Cross, where London Transport's East London line trains use a bay platform, the main line enters the shallow cutting that leads to St John's station. In steam days there were two island platforms here but one was removed in the early 1970s to make way for a single line spur, aimed at increasing rush hour capacity, coming down from the Lewisham flyover to join the main line. Just beyond the station the suburban line continues eastwards towards Blackheath while the four tracks of the main line curve away in a south-easterly direction, this being the start of the SER's cut off to Tonbridge, completed in 1868, to

*Top:*
**A view of the approach to London Bridge over the widened London and Greenwich Railway viaduct above the Thames flood plain. A London Midland Region 'Jinty' 0-6-0T is seen heading for Hither Green with a transfer freight from north London via Snow Hill. The dominance of the food industries in this part of London's inner suburbs is apparent in the view beyond the railway.** *David Lawrence*

*Above:*
**Hither Green engine shed opened in 1933 to serve the marshalling yards developed there since the end of the 19th century. In this view, taken on Saturday 2 May 1959, steam engines were still very much in evidence, but the depot had by then received an allocation of Sulzer Type 2 diesels on loan from the London Midland Region until the Southern's own Type 3 Cromptons were delivered.** *R. C. Riley*

shorten the London-Dover route (Chapter 1). Immediately beyond the junction the main line is crossed by the Lewisham fly-over. This was the scene of one of Britain's worst railway accidents when, on 4 December 1957, the 4.56pm Cannon Street-Ramsgate express, running over an hour late in thick fog, ran into the back of the 5.18pm Charing Cross-Hayes electric train. The force of the impact threw the leading coach and the tender of the engine, 'Battle of Britain' Pacific No 34066 *Spitfire,* against a pillar supporting the flyover, bringing it down on to the coaches. In all, 90 people were killed. A full account of the accident and a critique of the events before and after it took place have been written by Vaughan (*Obstruction Danger,* pp 116-129).

South of St John's are more railway junctions and housing dating from late Victorian and Edwardian times. By the time the line reaches Hither Green the scenery is dominated by railway installations and has been since the last years of the 19th century, when the SER began construction of a great marshalling yard. On the down side were sidings used mainly for exchange traffic between the Southern and other railway companies. This included not only the trains that came by way of Holborn Viaduct Low Level and Metropolitan Junction but others from the GWR, LNER and LMS that reached Hither Green by way of the West London line, the Catford loop and a number of new curves put in for the purpose in the late 1920s. The locomotive shed, therefore, usually contained a variety of 'foreign' engines; in addition to the types already mentioned, Stanier '8F' 2-8-0s came from Cricklewood while LNER 'J39' and 'J20' 0-6-0s arrived from Temple Mills in East London. For its share of the cross-London workings, Hither Green shed always had an allocation of the large 'W' class 2-6-4Ts built from 1931 for the purpose. The shed itself is a 1933 built structure with six roads situated in the triangle between the main line, the Dartford via Sidcup line and the Lee Junction spur. It lost its steam allocation in 1961 but remains active today housing diesels of BR's railfreight construction division.

Very late in the steam age a new depot was opened on the opposite side of the tracks for the handling of continental traffic, particularly fruit and vegetables, which had travelled via the Dover-Dunkirk train ferry. The trains were usually worked by Class 71 2500hp electric locos which changed from third rail to overhead power pickup in the sorting sidings outside the depot, a diesel shunting engine then propelling the vans into one of the two roads into the depot for unloading or transfer of the produce to road vehicles. At the peak of its prosperity Hither Green Continental Depot received up to four scheduled trains daily from Dover but the increasing use of road vehicles and the building of the new Nine Elms market reduced its usefulness. It was demolished in the late 1980s and a supermarket now occupies the site.

South of Hither Green is Grove Park, junction for the Bromley North branch, while the main line soon enters the cutting leading towards Elmstead Woods Tunnel, cut through the London Clay. The secluded station in the cutting beyond lies in a spacious residential district in great contrast to the closely packed 1920s and 1930s suburbia that surrounds the next two stations at Chislehurst and Petts Wood. The latter, lying south of the complex junctions which connect the LCDR and SER lines, is a good example of a suburb which grew around a station rather than an old village nucleus. The station opened in July 1928 following electrification of the lines to Victoria in 1925 and Charing Cross in 1926. In what had then been a sparsely populated area of fields and woods a building boom was stimulated which produced the 'drives', 'ways' and 'avenues' of detached and semi-detached houses and bungalows which surround the railway today. Orpington is another busy commuter station with four through platforms and two bays towards London. A four road electric depot and open air sidings replaced the two road steam shed here in the 1920s, although the main building of the latter, opened only in 1901, survives as railway offices.

South of Orpington the four tracks merge into two and the character of the line changes, for after crossing on a high embankment the dry upper part of the Cray Valley the railway enters a three mile cutting through the Chalk of the North Downs dip-slope. The line has been climbing steadily from New Cross but the gradient now steepens considerably and includes two miles at 1 in 120 before the summit of the Downs is reached just after Knockholt station. This and the other intermediate station at Chelsfield lie deep in the cutting and the rail traveller has little opportunity to appreciate the still relatively unspoilt scenery of woodlands and dry valleys on this high part of the Chalk plateau, which rises to over 600ft above sea level.

Through Polhill Tunnel the train gathers speed rapidly as it descends the escarpment. For those coming the other way the situation is very different for they face a continuous climb for three miles, much of it at 1 in 143, from Dunton Green to the summit just north of the tunnel. Over the years the signalmen at Polhill Intermediate Box must have witnessed many spectacular displays of fireworks, particularly at summer weekends when elderly goods engines and 4-4-0s on excursions and hop pickers' specials did battle with the bank.

As the train emerges from Polhill Tunnel a view of the Kentish Weald, with its oast houses and pastures opens out. Dunton Green still retains, on the up side, its SER wooden station building. From a separate platform on this side, between 1881 and 1961, the branch line train to Westerham shuttled backwards and forwards through the woods and pastures of the Gault Clay vale, serving Chevening Halt and Brasted on its four and three quarter-mile journey. In the 1930s the branch had over 20 trains each way on weekdays but towards the end of its life it became

*Above right:*
**South of Hither Green the Dover line passes through some of London's most attractive suburbs. A 'Schools' on the 5.17pm Cannon Street to Hastings is seen heading for Elmstead Woods tunnel, cut through the London Clay. On the up fast line a suburban electric unit, probably heading for London as empty stock, emerges from the tunnel.**
*R. C. Riley*

*Right:*
**South of Chislehurst is a complex series of junctions where numerous spurs join the former SER and LCDR main lines. The most southerly is Petts Wood Junction, where the loop from Bickley Junction joins the Dover line. 'Battle of Britain' Pacific No 34085 *501 Squadron* heads the 'Golden Arrow' on Saturday 16 May 1959 shortly after the junction had been altered in connection with the Kent coast electrification.**
*R. C. Riley*

*Below:*
**Orpington in the early days of Southern Railway electrification in the 1920s. The busy goods yard recalls one of the vanished features of country stations, while passing beneath the raised signalbox is a typical suburban train of the period consisting of two three-car units with former steam stock trailers between. The engine shed in the middle distance survives in use as offices to this day, but the rolling chalk downland of the upper Cray valley has long since disappeared beneath suburban housing.** *Revd A. W. V. Mace*

virtually a weekday rush-hour service only. Almost all trace of the branch has vanished and today the murderous traffic of the M25 motorway thunders along where once the little 'H' class tank and its two rail motor coaches passed their peaceful days.

Just before the train enters Sevenoaks station, once known as Sevenoaks (Tub's Hill), the LCDR line from Swanley curves in from the left, forming a valuable alternative lowland route from London through the Darent Valley. Electrification reached here in 1935, a regular interval service to London replacing the very infrequent local services that characterised most lines in Kent in steam days. Sevenoaks remained at the end of the third rail for over 25 years. South of the station the line enters another long damp cutting before entering the very wet Sevenoaks tunnel (at 3,451yds the longest on the SR) cut through the 700ft high crest of the Lower Greensand ridge. There follows a downhill sweep for over six miles through Hildenborough, where speeds of over 80mph are common, before the brakes go on as the train passes the playing fields of Tonbridge School and crosses the River Medway at the approach to the town. The severe curve before the station, by which the original 1842 line from Redhill is joined, has been eased several times to enable London bound trains not stopping at Tonbridge to gain a run at Hildenborough bank.

Eastwards the train gathers speed as it takes advantage of the long 25-mile straight, with only minor undulations, across the Vale of Kent to Ashford. This is the heart of the fruit belt and orchards and hop gardens are the dominant landscape features, both on the Weald Clay of the Vale and on the sandstone hills on each side. The area is also noted for its many surviving half-timbered farmhouses, some of them over 500 years old and contrasting sharply with the modern suburbia spreading out from the railway stations. Paddock Wood was, until the 1960s, a major centre for handling agricultural traffic, but the large warehouses on the north side of the station are today almost entirely road served. Once known as Maidstone Road it has been a junction since the Maidstone West branch opened in 1844. In later steam days the stations along this picturesque line through the Medway Valley were mainly served by 'H' class tanks with push and pull sets; many ran through to Tonbridge but today's electric trains generally use the down side bay. The less frequent trains on the line that climbed steeply into the Wealden hills at Hawkhurst waited in the bay platform on the up side; they then passed under the stilted signalbox before running parallel to the main line for almost a mile and curving away southwards. With its loop lines, branch line services and goods yards Paddock Wood was a busy station, especially in the hop-picking season. It remains busy today in a rather different role, serving the needs of the rather unattractive postwar commuter town on the south side of the line.

The wayside stations along the Vale of Kent retained their SER wooden buildings until all except those at Pluckley were removed in a rebuilding programme in the late 1980s. Headcorn was always the most interesting, for behind the up platform was another serving the northern end of the Kent & East Sussex line, one of the railway gems of southern England. To leave the

main line and cross the footbridge to the waiting branch line train, usually in the early 1950s a single LSWR low-roofed corridor with faded upholstery pulled by a rebuilt Stirling 'O1' class 0-6-0, was to step back to another age, where little had changed since the opening of the line in 1905. Some trains were mixed and passed the time shunting at wayside stations on the eight mile journey to Tenterden. But not everyone appreciated such delights and there was seldom more than two or three passengers. The line finally faded away on 2 January 1954 and today a thicket grows on the site of the exchange sidings and platform at Headcorn. Although the southern end of the KESR prospers as a preserved steam railway, land sales and building works make it a certainty that this end of the line has gone beyond recall.

South of Ashford, past Sevington where much of the aggregate for the building of the Eurotunnel site was handled in the late 1980s and early 1990s, there begins a steady climb of eight miles to Westenhanger, after which the journey is downhill all the way to Dover. The climb takes the line once again into the hills of the Lower Greensand. At Smeeth little remains of one of the very few closed stations on the Kentish main lines, closure to passenger traffic having taken place in 1954, before the era of large-scale

residential development in this area of south Kent. The main purpose of Westenhanger station, apart from a little commuter traffic, is to serve Folkestone racecourse, the former special racecourse platform now being disused. Between the short tunnels at Sandling and Saltwood lies the former Sandling Junction, a late addition to the stations on the line, opened in January 1888. The Tudor style buildings are attractively situated amid pinewoods; the well preserved remains of the Hythe branch platform, closed in December 1951, are clearly visible on the up side.

South of Saltwood Tunnel the landscape is dominated on the left by the Chalk escarpment and the western end of the Eurotunnel terminal, while at Cheriton the site of the junction with the former Elham Valley line to Canterbury can be discerned on the down side. Completed in 1889, this one time double track through the sparsely populated Chalk downs of East Kent was closed in 1940, although it found a new wartime role when heavy mobile guns were accommodated on the line as part of the front line defences. The end of the war brought about its final demise in June 1947 after a brief and unsuccessful attempt to restore passenger services at this southern end.

Between Cheriton and Folkestone Central the main line was quadrupled in the early 1960s to accommodate boat trains and the increase in domestic traffic that was expected to result from electrification. This brought about alterations both at Folkestone West (formerly Shorncliffe) and the Central station. The former, which handled heavy military traffic for the nearby camp, was quadruple tracked when the station was rebuilt in the 1880s and was distinguished until the 1960s rebuilding by a curious kink in the up platform. At Folkestone Central complete rebuilding took place, two island platforms capable of handling 12-coach trains replacing the former two through platforms. Fitting this layout in at a station built on a high embankment was a complex engineering task.

East of Folkestone Central there is a particularly fine view from the 100ft high Foord Viaduct over the town's Victorian terraces towards the harbour on the south side and the North Downs escarpment at Sugar Loaf and Castle Hill to the north. The steeply graded Harbour branch joins at the site of Folkestone Junction station, now closed to the public but still used as a staff halt. All boat trains reverse in the extensive sidings on the up side, the small engine shed which for over 60 years housed the

rebuilt Stirling 'R1' class 0-6-0Ts outstationed here from Dover for working boat trains up and down the 1 in 30 gradients being situated next to the down platform. East of Folkestone Junction the line enters the 532yd Martello Tunnel, crowned by one of the towers built as part of Britain's defences at the time of the Napoleonic Wars.

The line through the Warren along the base of the great Chalk cliffs is one of the most spectacular but difficult to maintain in Southern England. Its problems result from the geology of the area, for beneath the Chalk is a layer of Gault Clay, which holds up water percolating from above. A highly lubricated zone therefore builds up after wet weather until great masses of the Chalk slump forward forming an undercliff on the seaward side of the main cliff. It is through this unstable zone, where 12 major landslips were recorded between 1765 and 1937, that the railway passes. The most serious slip occured on 19 December 1915 when sideways movements distorted the track and pushed it out of alignment for over two miles, resulting in a train pulled by a 'D' class 4-4-0 being borne towards the sea. The line remained closed for the remainder of World War 1, all traffic having to use the former LCDR route to Dover. Abandonment of this section of line has been considered on a number of occasions and it remains to be seen if it will survive the changed traffic patterns resulting from the opening of the Channel Tunnel.

After leaving the Warren the line negotiates first Abbot's Cliff tunnel (1,933yd) and then that through Shakespeare Cliff (1,387yd), the latter of unconventional appearance with high Gothic arches at the twin single track tunnel mouths. The isolated mile or so between the tunnels has been the scene of two significant events in the last hundred years. In the late 19th century, when drilling took place here in an attempt to build a Channel Tunnel, seams of coal and iron ore were discovered and Dover Colliery, the first in east Kent, was opened on the seaward side of the railway. Nearly a century later most of the excavation for the Eurotunnel was carried out from the same site, the railway playing a vital role in delivering huge quantities of reinforced concrete segments for lining the tunnel. The reclaimed land at this point was made from spoil.

The final approach to Dover hugs the base of the cliffs which form the Western Heights, a low sea wall and the shingle bank protecting the railway from the waves. An extended freight yard now occupies the site of the original Dover Town passenger station and the steam shed where once Bulleid Pacifics and 'Britannias' were prepared to work the boat trains from the handsome station at Dover Marine. The main features of the station and harbour area are examined in Chapter 3.

*Above:*
**The main features of the Warren between Folkestone and Dover are seen in this photograph of one of the last steam hauled workings of the 'Golden Arrow' passing through in June 1961 behind rebuilt Bulleid Pacific No 34100 *Appledore.* Great masses of chalk slip down the face of the cliff to form an undercliff along which the railway runs. Despite much expenditure on measures to limit landslips and erosion, this remains one of the most difficult sections of the British Rail network to maintain.** *Mike Esau*

*Below:*
**The approach to Dover seen from above Shakespeare Cliff tunnel looking in an easterly direction. The great artificial harbour built by the Admiralty in the 19th century is clearly visible, Dover Marine station, the goods yard and the engine shed all being built on land reclaimed from the sea. Coal traffic from the local collieries is much in evidence in the foreground as a Standard Class 4 2-6-4T heads for Folkestone with an up local.** *Mike Esau*

## 2. Victoria to Dover

Situated within 10 minutes walk of Buckingham Palace, the LCDR's West End terminus at Victoria was originally two separate stations, one mainly used by the LBSCR and the other by the 'Chatham' and its partner, the Great Western. Until the formation of the SR there was no connection between them and passengers had to go outside to pass from one to another. The SR also renumbered the platforms in a single series from 1 to 17, but changes over the years have tended, if anything, to emphasise contrasts between the two sides. A distinguishing feature of the 'Brighton' side for many years was the great length of the platforms, created when the station was rebuilt longitudinally in the early 20th century and making it possible for two trains to be accommodated at one platform. Recent extension of the concourse has shortened them and the building of the Victoria Place shopping complex has made this side of the station above the platforms a very claustrophobic place. The 'Chatham' side, by contrast, remains little changed from steam days, its eight platforms under the twin-span arched roof still providing a light and airy environment.

Perhaps the most distinctive feature of Victoria in the years between its construction in the early 1860s and the end of the 19th century was the cosmopolitan nature of the trains using it. Along with Paddington, it was one of only two London terminals capable of handling broad gauge trains and regular services ran to Windsor and Southall via the West London Extension Railway. Services from the 'Chatham' side were also provided by the GNR to Barnet and the Midland to Finchley Road, while the LNWR, using the 'Brighton' side, ran trains to Willesden and Broad Street. These mainly ended just before World War 1 as bus, tram and tube railways were developed, although the GWR continued its lease on the 'Chatham' side until 1932. Until quite recently the faded lettering 'Great Western Railway' was still visible on the stone frontage of the station.

As these services ended Victoria assumed its role as London's main international station, with the decision of the newly formed SR in the early 1920s to concentrate boat train services for the short sea routes there rather than at Charing Cross, where space was more limited. Victoria thus became the 'Gateway to the Continent', by the 1930s the starting point for glam-

*Above right:*
**The severity of the climb out of Victoria up the 1 in 62 of Grosvenor bank is apparent in this view of 'Schools' class No 30914 *Eastbourne* departing on Saturday 19 May 1956. The clock on the face of the former British Overseas Airways terminal identifies the train as the 11.35am Victoria to Ramsgate. It includes four Pullman cars and later became the last train on the Thanet coast route to offer this facility.** *S. C. Nash*

*Right:*
**For some distance out of Victoria the Chatham line runs at a high level above the 'Battersea tangle' of railway lines. A down express is seen crossing the bridge over the entrance to Stewarts Lane shed. The lines on the bridge behind lead to Waterloo, and those behind 'King Arthur' No 30776 *Sir Galagars* to Clapham Junction and the West London line. To all this is now added the Stewarts Lane spur by which trains from the Channel Tunnel will reach Waterloo.** *R. C. Riley*

orous trains like the 'Golden Arrow' and the 'Night Ferry' and the station where crowned heads and presidents arrived on state visits. For a short time in the late 1930s trains were also operated to connect with Imperial Airways' flying boat services from Southampton. Victoria still remains the main starting point for journeys by the prestige VSOE Pullman train and VIP specials bringing visiting heads of state still arrive at platform 2 from Gatwick Airport. But the station's role as a terminus for boat trains is much diminished and will soon almost disappear when Channel Tunnel services use Waterloo. The compensation for Victoria is the growth of traffic on the Gatwick Express service from the 'Brighton' side to the world's second busiest international airport.

The start from Victoria presented steam engines with a problem as the line curves up a 1 in 62 gradient past Pimlico carriage sheds towards Grosvenor Bridge. The pilots which had brought in the empty carriages usually providing rear end assistance. They were usually 0-6-0 or 0-4-4 tanks or main line engines for a subsequent departure. Once over the bridge the line passes the former Battersea power station and swings away southeastwards over brick arches, leaving the traveller to gaze below on the right at the site of the pre-bridge terminus of Battersea Wharf and the last remains of the LBSCR's Battersea roundhouse, overshad-

*Above left:*
**A fine view is provided from the arches beyond the bridge into the yard of Stewarts Lane shed, which still survives as a diesel depot. Apart from a small diesel shunter, No 11220, steam still dominated the scene when this picture was taken on Sunday 5 April 1959. The 0-6-0T on coal pilot duty is an LBSCR 'E2' class, frequently used on empty stock duties at Victoria.** *R. C. Riley*

*Above:*
**Stewarts Lane yard from the opposite end, featuring one of the former LBSCR overhead electric units dating from 1909 crossing the South London line viaduct towards Battersea Park station with a London Bridge to Victoria local service. The large mechanical coaling plant was provided in the 1930s when Stewarts Lane was rebuilt to permit the closure of the former LBSCR Battersea shed. In evidence near the coaling stage are 'D' class 4-4-0 No 31574 and a pannier tank which had probably arrived with a train for the Western Region goods depot at South Lambeth.** *J. J. Smith*

*Below:*
**At Factory Junction the West London line (bottom left) which still carries inter-regional passenger and freight trains, joins the Chatham route. Against a background of Battersea Power Station, Bulleid Pacific No 34099 *Lynmouth* passes on Sunday 19 September 1954 with a Ramsgate express, while 'H' class No 31263 has come up from Stewarts Lane to run light to Ashford works.** *R. C. Riley*

owed by the gas holder. It closed in 1933, when the remaining engines were transferred to Stewarts Lane.

The Chatham line is now in the heart of the 'Battersea tangle' of railway lines. It crosses the LSWR route into Waterloo at a high level, with the new spur for international trains curving down to the left. To the right there is a view down to the yard of Stewarts Lane engine shed, rebuilt in the 1930s with 16 roads and a tall concrete coaling plant beside the South London line viaduct. With an allocation of over 100 engines ranging from Bulleid Pacifics and 'Britannias' down to small tank engines, it formerly provided power not only for the Kent lines but also services on the non-electrified tracks to Oxted and the former LBSCR lines beyond. Closed to steam in September 1963, the now roofless shed is still the home of a fleet of diesel and electro-diesel locomotives and has a large shed for multiple units and other coaching stock, including the VSOE Pullmans, nearby.

Beyond Stewarts Lane the line passes Factory Junction where in steam days through trains like the 'Sunny South Special' and excursions from the Midlands joined the Kent coast route from the West London line. The main line is paralleled through Wandsworth Road and Clapham by the South London line, for 20 years, until 1929 electrified using the LBSCR's overhead system until this was abandoned by the SR in favour of the third rail.

Amid the Victorian terraces at Brixton the main line takes the right hand fork to part company with the Catford loop line to Shortlands. Allegedly built because of fears of the collapse of Penge Tunnel, the loop provided in steam days a valuable relief route out of London at times of heavy traffic and is still used today as a diversionary route when the main line is closed for maintenance work. The line from Blackfriars joins on the left at Herne Hill, where once LCDR boat trains joined and split their West End and City portions. Herne Hill was also the site of a large sorting yard where goods trains from north of the Thames were remarshalled for forwarding to yards in Kent; situated alongside the Blackfriars line, its site is now a council depot.

From here to the tunnel at Sydenham Hill the line climbs at 1 in 101 past the grounds of Dulwich College. After penetrating the London Clay of the Crystal Palace ridge in Penge Tunnel (2,200yd), it ducks under the Brighton main line from London Bridge and drops through Penge East, a comparatively unspoilt LCDR station fitting well into the wooded landscape of this attractive area of south east London.

At Shortlands, the former Bromley station, the Catford loop rejoins the main line and quadruple tracks extend for about seven miles to Swanley. Most Kent coast expresses stop at Bromley South and the climb at 1 in 95 towards Bickley and the point where the SER main line passes overhead always gave steam trains a slow start. At Bickley Junction boat trains usually fork right to join the SER route at Petts Wood Junction. By now the 1930s suburban landscape has been left behind and the line passes through heathlands similar to those of west Surrey, developed on the sands of the Blackheath Beds.

Beyond Bickley there begins the series of undulations that characterise this main line as it crosses the valleys of the streams draining the Chalk dip-slope towards the Thames estuary. The first drop takes the line into the industrialised Cray Valley, crossed on a long viaduct, before climbing again to Swanley, junction for the Sevenoaks and Ashford via Maidstone East line. The original station straddled the junction east of the present one, opened when the line was electrified in 1939. The four-track section ends here and from the footplate a splendid vista opens up as the line sweeps down for over three miles at 1 in 100 into the Darent Valley. On this high speed stretch of line, constrained only by the 80mph limit at the Chatham end of Farningham Road viaduct, the exploits of Driver Sam Gingell on the 'D1' and 'E1' 4-4-0s in the 1950s became something of a legend.

From Farningham Road viaduct, with its views of the paper mills and ponds along the Darent Valley, the line climbs again across the Chalk plateau to Sole Street. Just short of Longfield the bed of the double-track LCDR branch to Gravesend West curves away to the left at what used to be Fawkham Junction. Opened in 1886 it passed through a sparsely populated area but once carried boat trains, usually a 'C' class 0-6-0 and three or four coaches, from Victoria bound for Gravesend Pier and the Batavier Line connection to Rotterdam. When they ceased early in World War 2 the importance of the line diminished; an 0-4-4T and two coaches usually providing the service, which had become something of a steam island in the otherwise mainly electrified area of north Kent. The number of trains dwindled to only about five each way on most days and closure to passenger traffic took place from 3 May 1953. Freight traffic, on the other hand, was heavy since this line handled most of the goods bound for Gravesend, leaving the SER station to handle most of the passengers. It continued until 1967, the southern end of the line subsequently reopening between 1972 and 1976 to carry coal to Southfleet for use in the cement industry.

After Sole Street station there begins the descent into the major gap cut by the River Medway through the North Downs, a view of the valley with its industries, bridges and shipping opening up to the right. To steam trains heading for the Kent coast the descent of Sole Street bank provided an opportunity for the fireman to rest but the vicious reverse curve, with a 30mph speed limit, at the foot of the bank as the line approaches Rochester Bridge, restricted the potential for high speed. It also gave westbound trains no opportunity to take a run at the five mile climb at 1 in 100 to Sole Street. The curve was even sharper until 1927, when it was eased by diverting the main line on to the former SER bridge which originally carried their expensive and short lived branch to Chatham Central over the river. The complex history of the railways around Rochester and the links between the LCDR main line and the SER line from Strood to Maidstone through the Medway Valley has been outlined by White (H.P. White, *Forgotten Railways: South East England*. pp 118-121). Little remains today of some of the lines he discusses, although at the approach to the twin platforms of the present Rochester station a large expanse of derelict land on the left marks the site of the former Chatham goods depot.

Beyond Rochester the main line enters the first of the three Medway towns tunnels by which it negotiates the conurbation spread over the Chalk hills east of the river. The first is Fort Pitt tunnel (428yd), followed by Chatham Tunnel (297yd), with the station sandwiched between them. This has two through platforms but was once a double island with a goods depot and a turntable. Beyond Chatham Tunnel the line climbs at 1 in 135 over Luton arches to Gillingham Tunnel to reach the station, once called New Brompton and serving the easternmost of the

Medway towns. Gillingham is also the 'railway town' of the area. The now vanished three road engine shed, closed in 1960, stood on the up side east of the station, its allocation of about 30 engines consisting mainly of 4-4-0s, 0-6-0s and 0-4-4Ts for local duties. For 20 years from 1939 Gillingham was the terminus for electric trains from London and there is still a large depot for multiple units here. The branch to Chatham dockyard trails in on the left hand side. After seeing little use for many years it enjoyed something of a revival in the early 1990s, trainloads of contaminated soil from a land reclamation project being sent for dumping in old brick pits on the Bedford-Bletchley line.

*Below:*
**The 2.09pm stopping train to Faversham and Dover waits at what was formerly the down island platform at Chatham during the last weekend of steam working in 1959, headed by 'L' class No 31779.** *J. J. Smith*

*Bottom:*
**South of Faversham the LCDR Dover line begins to climb into the orchard country around Selling and Canterbury. Although still used by the Continental expresses, most of the trains on this line in the later days of steam were locals connecting with Thanet expresses at Faversham, as depicted here with 'L' class No s1772 on a Dover to Faversham train.** *Revd A. W. V. Mace*

*Above:*
A view of the London end of the now vanished spur linking the LCDR line west of Canterbury East with the SER line through Canterbury. The spur was opened and closed three times between World War 1 and 1955. Following the east coast floods early in 1953, it was restored to link Thanet with London while the route via Herne Bay was closed. 'Schools' No 30922 *Marlborough* is seen leaving the spur with a Birchington-Victoria express during this time. Canterbury Cathedral is in the far right background. *Revd A. W. V. Mace*

*Right:*
Another vanished spur, the Kearsney loop, connected the Faversham and Dover line with the Dover and Deal Joint line, forming a triangle just north of Dover. It also saw use in the 1953 flood emergency and by special trains such as this annual Snowdown Colliery miners' excursion to Margate, seen disturbing the rusty rails on Thursday 6 August 1953. Because trains coming off the loop were unable to take a run at the 1 in 70 bank to Martin Mill, 'N' class No 31850 had been provided as pilot to No 34067 *Tangmere. A. F. Mercer*

The mainly level section through orchards and market gardens towards Rainham and Newington has changed significantly since electrification in 1959. The line between these two stations was quadrupled to cater for the expected traffic increase and in the case of Rainham this has certainly materialised, turning what was in steam days a quiet country station with an infrequent service into a major commuting centre surrounded by extensive housing estates. East of Newington the line rises steeply on Bobbing bank before dropping again past the triangular junction for the Sheerness branch, serving a major industrial area of north Kent and still busy with freight traffic.

Sittingbourne station, formerly Sittingbourne and Milton Regis, has an island platform on the down side and a single platform on the up, the outer face of the former still being used by the Sheerness branch trains. There was once an all-over roof, removed in the 1950s. In the past goods sidings on each side of the line served this important industrial town and those on the down side remain, receiving bulk tankers loaded with china clay from Cornwall and other materials for the Bowater paper mills. Another depot alongside the platform receives tankers of starch from Manchester.

The line is fairly level through the orchards to Teynham. At Ospringe there is evidence of brickmaking, once a staple industry of the Faversham area, the works being served by private sidings trailing in on the down side. The well preserved Victorian station at Faversham is a product of rebuilding in 1897. At this time the former Preston Street level crossing was replaced by a diversionary road and an underbridge, the road being called Forbes Road, after the LCDR's Chairman. Other aspects of Faversham's railway history are discussed in Chapter 3.

Between Faversham and Canterbury the former LCDR main line to Dover traverses one of Kent's major fruit growing areas, the orchards and hop gardens thriving on the sheltered south facing London Clay upland of the Blean. The railway is frequently either in shallow cuttings through the Brickearth soils or on embankments, the latter offering especially attractive views during blossom time in April and May. In steam days the intermediate station at Selling was a major centre for fruit traffic, sidings on both sides of the line providing storage and loading for vans destined for the London market.

After leaving Ensden Tunnel (629yd) the line begins its descent to the crossing of the Stour Valley on the western outskirts of Canterbury. From the Dover line a view opens up to the south across the orchards to the SER line from Ashford to Ramsgate through Canterbury West following the valley floor. Just east of the crossing of the two lines is the site of the spur by which on three occasions they have been joined. Connection was first made during World War 1, when a double line, much used by munitions trains to Richborough, was provided. It closed in 1920 and the track and junctions at each end were removed in 1936 although the signalboxes were left intact. A single line connection was restored at the start of World War 2 and saw use by armoured trains but it again fell into disuse when peace was restored, the track being left *in situ* but with the connections at each end taken out. The east coast floods of early 1953 again provided an opportunity for the spur to show its worth when breaches in the sea wall along the north Kent coast put the main

*Below:*
**Canterbury East station in 1958, with its all-over roof in process of being dismantled. The Faversham to Dover line was included in the first phase of the Kent Coast electrification, and conductor rails are in place as 'L' class No 31768 pauses with a down train.** *P. Ransome Wallis*

*Right:*
**The scene at Shepherdswell, former junction for the East Kent Light Railway, in April 1959 with No 34066 *Spitfire* heading an up boat train out of the tunnel, the longest on the LCDR. By this time the remains of the EKLR survived only as the Tilmanstone Colliery branch, and the train on the right consists of coal traffic awaiting collection by a main line engine.**
*Gerald Siviour*

*Below right:*
**South of Shepherdswell tunnel the line emerges into the Lydden valley, leading southwards to the Dour valley, cut deep into the high chalk plateau of the North Downs. 'N' class No 31819 is seen starting the descent towards Dover with a mixed freight in 1959.** *Gerald Siviour*

line to Thanet out of action for four months. The Canterbury spur was hastily restored with double track during February and became part of the main line from London to Thanet via Faversham, a route two miles shorter to Ramsgate than by the coast. With fewer stops cuts in journey times became possible, although Margate passengers had appreciably longer journeys. When the emergency ended the use of the spur again ceased and it was finally removed in 1955.

At the approach to Canterbury there is a splendid view of the cathedral and the medieval wall before the train enters the East station. Although its former all-over roof was dismantled in 1958 many original LCDR features remain, notably the signalbox on tall stilts still controlling a number of semaphore signals.

South of Canterbury the Dover line climbs out of the Stour Valley on to the dip-slope of the North Downs. Beyond Bekesbourne the orchards die out and are replaced by a mainly arable landscape, deep beneath which coal mining took place for most of the first 80 years of this century. The remains of Snowdown Colliery can be seen on the east side of the line. Opened in 1908 it was the second largest in Kent in terms of its output and from the extensive sidings, once shunted by the Avonside 0-6-0Ts *St Dunstan* and *St Thomas*, up to eight freight trains a day were scheduled to depart in the 1950s. The last purpose of these sidings following closure of the colliery after the 1984/5 pit strike, was to dispatch trains of mine waste to Sevington for building of the

foundations of the Eurotunnel terminal at Cheriton. Snowdown and Nonington Halt was opened on 1914 to serve the miners who travelled mainly from Dover, while to the north stands what was to have been the model village of Aylesham, created in the 1920s to house families moving into Kent from older coalfields. Further evidence of the Kent coalfield could also once be seen at Shepherdswell, with perhaps a glimpse in the sidings of a rebuilt Stirling 'O1' class 0-6-0 on a train from the Tilmanstone Colliery branch, the last active remnant of the East Kent Light Railway.

Leaving Shepherdswell Tunnel, at 2,376yd the longest on the LCDR, the railway encounters the totally different landscape of the dry upper part of the Lydden Valley. It is cut very deep into the Chalk plateau and its steep sides support mainly pasture and woodlands. The suburbs of Dover reach out to Kearsney, where the up platform was once an island used by five or six trains a day to Deal via the steeply-graded loop to the Dover and Deal Joint line, opened in 1881. By the 1930s the Kearsney loop, whose remains are still just visible a mile south of the station, had largely fallen into disuse, connection for Deal line trains being made at Dover Priory. Like the Canterbury loop it enjoyed a brief return to glory during the early days of the 1953 flood emergency, Thanet trains making a long detour this way before the Canterbury loop was restored. In the early 1960s it was electrified to allow coal trains to pass this way to Richborough power station.

*Above:*

**East Kent experiences an almost continental climate and snowfall can be heavy. In January 1957 'King Arthur' No 30767 *Sir Valence* leaves Herne Bay with a down Ramsgate express in wintry conditions. In later years snow on the conductor rails caused considerable problems for the third rail electric trains, requiring steam or diesel locomotives to go to their rescue.** *Brian Coates*

*Below:*

**The scene near Dumpton Park north of Ramsgate, where the present route branches off from the old main line to Ramsgate Harbour. This closed in 1926 and its remains are seen to the right of Eastern Region 'B1' No 61138, passing with the 10.35am Victoria to Ramsgate while on loan during the 1953 locomotive crisis (Chapter 10). On the skyline is St Lawrence College in Thanet which gave its name to 'Schools' 4-4-0 No 30934.** *S. C. Nash*

*Above:*
**The country junction at Minster in early BR days. The route straight ahead is the SER line to Ramsgate, with the former Deal branch on the right. A third side to the triangle is made by a spur which enabled Kent coast expresses to bypass Minster. A train of coal from local collieries is headed by 'C' class No 31690.** *Revd A. W. V. Mace*

Dover Priory is entered by way of two short tunnels. The original station had an over-all roof but the present one, with its long single platform and an island dates from a major reconstruction in 1932. Dover engine shed was also once located here; it remained in use until 1932, despite the building in 1928 of a new one in a less cramped but more exposed position on the sea front near the Marine station.

## 3. The coastal route - Faversham to Dover via Thanet

It has already been shown that the two main lines between London and Dover came into being in a very piecemeal fashion. This is even more true of the coastal section from Faversham to Dover, used since the 1920s as a part of a circular route for the 'rounders' - trains which made a tour round Kent on a Charing Cross-Dover-Ramsgate-Margate-Victoria itinerary.

The coastal route developed from four different lines built in the mid 19th century; they were subsequently connected to each other and to the rest of the system over a lengthy period, so that the through route was not finally completed until July 1926. The section between Faversham and a point north-east of Dumpton Park originated as the LCDR's Thanet branch opened in stages between Faversham and Ramsgate Harbour and completed in 1863. From Dumpton Park to a point west of the present Ramsgate station is the newest section of the line, the spur opened by the SR in 1926 to link the LCDR line to the SER's Ramsgate Town branch from Ashford completed in 1846 (Fig 5). Upon its completion the two earlier stations, along with the branch to Margate Sands, were closed. West of Ramsgate the Ashford line is followed as far as a point east of the small town of Minster, where a sharply curved spur connects with the SER's Minster-Deal branch opened in 1847. The final section of the coast route to the junction with the direct Faversham-Dover line at Buckland Junction near Dover, originated as the Dover and Deal Joint line (LCDR and SER). As the following paragraphs show, this varied history of the route is equalled by its geographical diversity.

From Faversham the Thanet line runs northeastwards to its first encounter with the coastal marshes of east Kent as it heads for Whitstable. To the north the view extends over the

pastures and drainage dikes of the Graveney marshes to the mudflats of the Swale estuary, with the Isle of Sheppey beyond. Southwards the land rises gently to the wooded uplands of the Blean, its slopes covered in orchards as are some of the islands of London Clay rising out of the marshes.

The railway reaches the coast amid the seaside bungalows and chalets of Seasalter and in the following ten miles across the London Clay to Reculver passes through one of the most urbanised coastal strips in southern England, all in great contrast to the sparsely populated inland area of the Blean. In the interwar years this area continued to develop as one of London's long-distance commuter settlements and the contribution of the railway to this is discussed in Chapter 5. The roads radiating from the stations, as in some of London's outer suburbs, testify to the importance of the railway in facilitating this growth, and in 1930 the SR opened the new halt at Chestfield and Swalecliffe to cater for expanding traffic. Its wooden waiting shelters and platforms testify to the age of economy in which it was constructed. In more recent years electrification provided a further spur to population growth on this part of the Kent coast and many rows of modern bungalows were added to the earlier urbanisation.

From Herne Bay the line descends past Reculver to cross the reclaimed marshlands of the Wantsum Channel, which once cut off the Isle of Thanet from the mainland. Reclamation here was partly by natural silting and partly as a result of the work of monks in the middle ages. The last ship to use the Wantsum Channel did so in 1672 and reclamation was virtually completed by the closing of the sea wall between Birchington and Reculver in 1808. The railway runs very close to this wall for about three miles and it was along this stretch that major breaches were made during the disastrous floods of 31 January 1953, resulting in the line here being closed for nearly four months. Vast quantities of Chalk was carried by special trains from Knockholt and Ramsgate; new sea walls and flood control

**When the lines in Thanet were remodelled in the 1920s, through running from Dover to Ramsgate became general and Deal lost much of its importance. Its engine shed closed in 1930, although the building remained in use when this picture was taken over 20 years later. A London Midland Region 2-6-4T is seen in the background on a local train passing the 1930s style signalbox, which remains in use to this day.** *LPC No K4005/Ian Allan Ltd*

installations were provided to reduce waterlogging and today much of the marshland is under arable cultivation.

East of Birchington the railway climbs to reach the Chalk upland of the former Isle of Thanet, characterised by its built up coastline and the open, highly cultivated landscape of the interior, where the growing of vegetables in large open fields has long been a major activity. Their accessibility by water from London and a reputation for a sunny, bracing climate made Margate and Ramsgate important resorts over a century before the coming of the railway but there is no doubt that railways did much to enhance their prosperity and encourage residential development. The vast excursion traffic from all over the south of England and the Midlands, but from south east London in particular, was a great source of interest to railway enthusiasts. The main stations at Margate and Ramsgate remain today fine examples of SR architecture of the 1920s, although the smaller ones at Westgate and Birchington retain many LCDR features.

West of Ramsgate the line descends towards Minster marshes, the eastern end of the former Wantsum Channel. Approaching Minster trains from Dover take the eastern side of the triangular junction leading to the former Deal branch. In steam days they sometimes ran into Minster, the engine running round before continuing the journey southwards via the western side of the triangle. This is little used today and has been reduced to a single track. Twice in this century the marshes surrounding the mouth of the Stour have been a scene of developments temporarily providing a great deal of railway traffic. During World War 1 the great military port of Richborough, complete with train ferry and marshalling yard was built here and around 30 engines operated in the extensive sidings. After the war its use declined and a proposal by Pearson and Dorman Long to build a steelworks using Kent coal and imported iron ore came to nothing. Today the marshlands are dominated by the triple cooling towers of Richborough power station, opened in 1963 to provide a use for Kent coal following loss of the railway market as a result of electrification. Later it was converted to burn other fuels and trainloads of oil arrived from the Isle of Grain. This has now ceased and the extensive sidings have been disconnected from the main line.

The former Deal branch continues southwards across the market gardens of the Lydden Valley marshlands. At the approach to the town the two mile line to Betteshanger Colliery, the largest in the Kent coalfield, turned off to the right. Opened in 1924 the colliery was the only one in Kent to survive the 1984/5 miners' strike and continued to dispatch rail traffic until its closure in 1989. At the end of its life coal was carried by conveyer to a loading point on the branch and little remained of the extensive sidings where up to six steam shunters once worked. Little remains at Deal station, either, to indicate its former importance as a terminus. The southbound platform is the original and the station once had an all-over roof, the present space between the tracks being occupied by a siding, later converted to a through road when the Dover and Deal line opened. Deal once boasted an engine shed (closed in 1930 when the new one at Ramsgate opened), carriage sidings and a busy goods yard, but today only the large 1930s style SR signalbox hints at past glories.

The remaining eight miles to Dover contain some of the steepest gradients on the Kent coast as the line climbs from sea level at Deal to nearly 350ft at the northern portal of Guston Tunnel. On the section to Martin Mill it makes use of the shallow open valleys of the Chalk dip-slope but the descent through the tunnel and round the great semicircle across the Dour Valley to join the Faversham-Dover line is mainly on gradients of around 1 in 70. It was a section of line which presented a considerable obstacle to northbound trains in steam days and banking was frequently necessary especially when heavy trains went this way, for example after the 1953 floods. Certainly the speed of trains out of Dover gave passengers plenty of time to appreciate the splendid view southwards towards the castle and the harbour as they clambered up the side of the Dour Valley on to the high, windswept plateau of the North Downs.

# Chapter 3

# Principal junctions and traffic centres

## Tonbridge

Tonbridge (known as Tunbridge until 1852, Tunbridge Junction until 1893 and then Tonbridge Junction until 1929) derived its importance in steam days from its location at a focal point of lines in west Kent, where main line trains halted to connect with stopping trains to and from Redhill, Hastings, Maidstone West and Ashford. Local services also reached the town from the former LBSCR lines in East Sussex via the single line connection between Grove Junction, south of Tunbridge Wells Central on the Hastings line, and Tunbridge Wells West, while engines for the Hawkhurst and Westerham branches were also provided from Tonbridge. A further manifestation of its importance as a meeting point of routes was the provision of two goods yards, one to the east of the station with a large goods shed dealing mainly with local traffic and another (where trains were marshalled) situated to the west alongside the Redhill line. The west yard still survives, being used by engineers' department trains.

    The layout presented severe operating problems in steam days and over the years several attempts were made to resolve them. The sharp curve at the western end of the station was a handicap to London trains facing the six mile climb to Hildenborough and to ease the necessary speed restriction, remodelling of the layout was carried out in the 1930s and again in 1958. At the eastern end Hastings trains, leaving the single down platform, have to cross a complex network of up and down tracks before facing the sharply curved and steep climb (some of it at 1 in 53) towards Somerhill Tunnel and Tunbridge Wells. It was to reduce the need for such a steep gradient that the junction of the main and Hastings lines originally faced eastwards and the remains of this alignment are still visible.

Tonbridge engine shed stood in the angle between the Hastings and Dover lines, parallel with the latter. It had two sections, one with three through roads and the other with one through and one short track. At the rear was an open area, known as the 'gardens', where surplus engines were often held in store. Typical pre- and post- World War 2 allocations were:

**1 October 1937**
'C' class 0-6-0: 1037, 1086, 1219, 1225/7/9, 1481, 1513, 1590/3, 1682.
'O1' class 0-6-0: 1048, 1123, 1371/2, 1396, 1432/7.
'D' class 4-4-0: 1057, 1488, 1490, 1577, 1586, 1591, 1730/3/7, 1740/2/6, 1750.
'H' class 0-4-4T: 1182, 1193, 1276/9, 1309, 1310, 1324, 1512, 1520, 1553.
'R1' class 0-4-4T: 1704/7.
'R1' class 0-6-0T: 1069.
'N1' class 2-6-0: 1822, 1879, 1880.
'D1' class 0-4-2T: 2224, 2355.
'E4' class 0-6-2T: 2496, 2560/4.

*Below:*
**A view eastwards from Tonbridge early in the morning on 30 October 1980, featuring the penultimate up 'Night Ferry' headed by Crompton diesel No 33043. The Hastings line diverges to the right in the middle distance, the engine shed once standing in the angle with the main line. In this picture the east goods depot is still busy with parcels vans. Although it has now disappeared, a great deal of mail traffic is still handled at Tonbridge.** *D. Benn*

**20 July 1953**

'C' class 0-6-0: 31037/8, 31219, 31244, 31270/2/7, 31585/8, 31590, 31716/7.
'D' class 4-4-0: 31729, 31733/4.
'D1' class 4-4-0: 31727.
'H' class 0-4-4T: 31164, 31177, 31184, 31193, 31239, 31259, 31261, 31523, 31530, 31548, 31554.
'R' class 0-4-4T: 31666.
'R1' class 0-4-4T: 31698, 31703/4.
'L' class 4-4-0: 31760-6, 31770/1/3.
'E4' class 0-6-2T: 32503, 32578, 32580.
'Q1' class 0-6-0: 33026-36.

Thus in its heyday the shed had an allocation of over 50 engines. It remained remarkably constant in composition, consisting of 0-4-4Ts for the mainly push-and-pull operated branch lines, pregrouping 0-6-0s for local goods work, 4-4-0s cascaded from the main line for stopping trains and 0-6-2Ts mainly for shunting in the yards. The only postgrouping engines allocated were 2-6-0s in the 1930s, replaced by 'Q1' class 0-6-0s in the post-

war era; both mainly worked heavy freight trains between Tonbridge and the other marshalling yards in Kent (Ch.9). The passing years had little impact on the life of these country engine sheds and the fact that so much traffic was reliably carried year in and year out was a great tribute to the men and the elderly engines that worked it.

Tonbridge shed took a long time to die. It outlived electrification of the main line by continuing to service engines (mainly Standard 2-6-4Ts) for the Redhill and former LBSCR lines: it lost its own allocation in June 1962 and finally closed in January 1965. Even then diesels continued to stable on the site and remnants of the building survived well into the 1980s.

## Ashford

Ashford is a classic railway town, still the meeting point of three secondary lines (from Maidstone, Hastings and Ramsgate) with the London-Dover route. In the heyday years it had extensive freight yards east and west of the station, an engine shed with an allocation of around 50 and workshops employing more than 3,000 men to build and maintain the locomotives and rolling

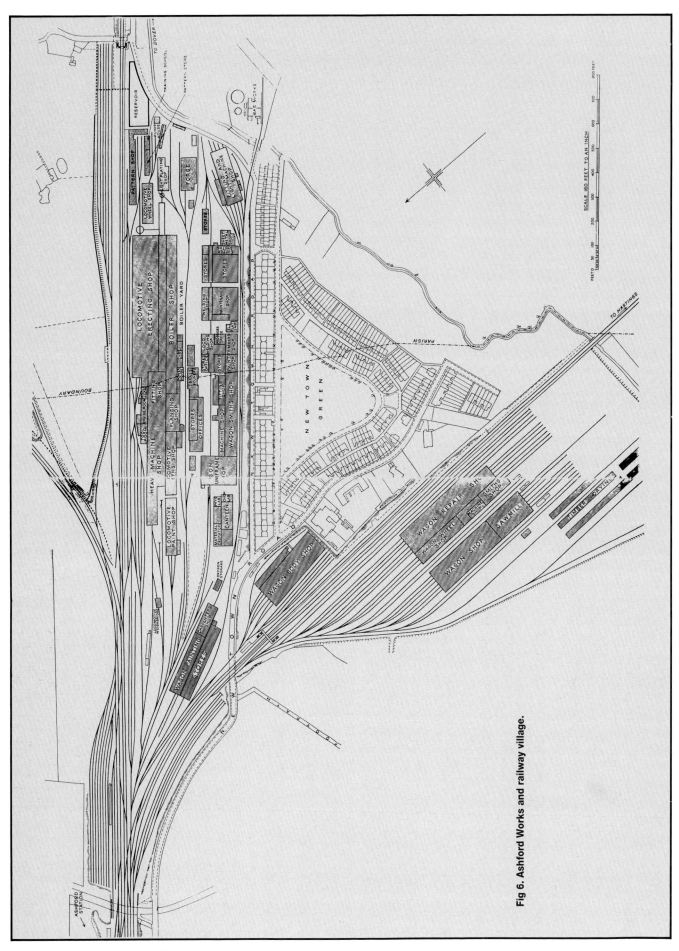

Fig 6. Ashford Works and railway village.

stock used in Kent. The latter was surrounded by the railway village south east of the old market town on the opposite side of the main line. In it, names like Stirling Road, Wainwright Place and Maunsell Place still to this day commemorate some of the great names of Ashford's railway past.

The SER decided in 1845 to establish its main works here, where land was cheap, to replace facilities it previously shared with the London and Croydon and Brighton companies at New Cross. A site of 185 acres was acquired and the locomotive works opened in 1847, producing its first new engines in 1853; in 1850 a carriage and wagon works was added. To accommodate the workforce the settlement at first known as Alfred Town was established around a central green (Fig 6). Its features included a bath house, whose water tank also supplied the works, a shop, a public house and later a school. A Mechanics Institute, the bastion of 19th century adult education, also thrived. The first houses were back to back dwellings, with rents based upon the means of the tenants. A mansion called Alfred House was provided for the Locomotive Superintendent, other housing being provided to reflect the grade of the employees.

Ashford's greatest days as a locomotive works probably began in 1878, with the arrival, as Superintendent, of James Stirling, brother of Patrick of GNR fame, a true Victorian autocrat and disciplinarian. Domeless engines with almost open footplates, spartan even by the standards of those days, were his hallmark, along with a policy of standardisation. His 'F' class 4-4-0s, introduced in 1883, contributed to a great speeding up of services, being capable of running boat trains from London to Dover in just over 90 minutes. One of them, No 240 *Onward*, distinguished itself by winning a gold medal at the 1889 Paris exhibition. A total of 88 of these engines were built, most later being converted to 'F1s', with raised boilers and extended smokeboxes.

Stirling was succeeded in 1898 by another of the great names of British locomotive history, Harry S. Wainwright, who had already established a reputation for fine coaches during his stewardship of the carriage works. Many superlatives have been

*Above:*
**The approach to Ashford from the west, with the line from Maidstone East joining the Tonbridge line by the signalbox in the distance. The 10.35am Maidstone East to Minster local train is seen on 3 October 1959 headed by London Midland Region 2-6-4T No 42078, built at Brighton. Ashford's livestock market is one of the largest in Britain and once provided a great volume of rail traffic.** *Revd A. W. V. Mace*

*Below:*
**The busy freight yards at the eastern end of Ashford station on Saturday 14 May 1955 with 'L' class No 31762 making an unusual sight on a lightweight freight taking the Canterbury line. The site of these yards may in due course accommodate Ashford International station, served by Channel Tunnel expresses.** *D. Penny*

used to describe Wainwright's handsome and stylish engines, the product of a close working relationship with the chief draughtsman, Robert Surtees. With their graceful curving splashers, polished brass domes and copper capped chimneys the 'D' class 4-4-0s, introduced in 1901, epitomised the new era on the railways of Kent after the years of pennypinching resulting from competition between the SER and the LCDR. A new livery of Brunswick green (lined out with light green, yellow and red), black and vermilion with dark red underframes replaced Stirling's austere black. Other equally fine 4-4-0s followed in the form of the 'E' and 'L' classes, some of the latter being assembled in the works from parts made in Germany in the last weeks before the outbreak of World War 1. These and the other Wainwright classes like the 'C' 0-6-0s, of which 109 were built, and the 'H' 0-4-4Ts (64) were, like the Stirling engines before them, distinguished by their extreme longevity, some of them lasting to the end of steam in Kent.

In 1912, just before the end of the Wainwright era, Ashford works itself underwent a major transformation to accommodate a 50% increase in its workload resulting from closure of the LCDR factory at Longhedge in south London. A new erecting shop 580ft long capable of dealing with up to 28 engines at a time was constructed along with new tender and paint shops, all close to and parallel with the Dover line. At this time the locomotive running sheds were also on this side of the main line, along with the Klondyke wagon works. The Kimberley works lay on the far side of the Hastings line. To accommodate the additional workforce arriving from London, 126 new houses with up to six rooms each were built in New Town, many of them still remaining today.

The coming of war almost coincided with the arrival of a new Locomotive Superintendent, Richard Maunsell, from the Great Southern and Western Railway of Ireland. Many things changed. Gone was Wainwright's elegant livery, giving way to wartime grey, but in 1917 the works produced its prototype six-coupled express engine, 'K' class 2-6-4T No 790, along with its first mixed/traffic mogul No 810. Carriage work ceased at Ashford on formation of the SR and was concentrated at Eastleigh and Lancing. Wagon and locomotive building continued, however, although some important work like the rebuilding of some of the 'D' and 'E' classes with raised boilers and Belpaire fireboxes as the 'D1' and 'E1' classes was contracted to the outside firm of Beyer Peacock.

The main contribution of Ashford to the locomotive construction programme in the 1930s was the building of Maun-

*Above left:*
**The rural nature of the area in which Ashford Works was built is apparent in this early 20th Century view, Newtown Road, leading to the railway village, being little more than a country lane. The clock tower still stands, guarding the entrance to the industrial estate which the works became when most of it closed to railway activity in 1981.**
*Kent Arts and Libraries*

*Above:*
**On 20 October 1926 Ashford Works received Royal visitors. The Duke and Duchess of York (later King George VI and Queen Elizabeth (the Queen Mother)) are seen boarding the footplate of the then new No 850 *Lord Nelson*, accompanied by its designer, Richard Maunsell.**
*Kent Arts and Libraries*

*Below:*
**A part of Ashford Works erecting shop in the late 1950s showing how labour-intensive railway work was in the steam age, over 3,000 men once being employed at Ashford on the building and maintenance of engines and rolling stock. Under repair are 'U' class 2-6-0 No 31632 and 'L1' No 31754. Although closed to steam operations for about 30 years, Ashford erecting shop remains in use today for the repair of cranes and track maintenance vehicles.** *Mike Esau*

sell moguls and the 'W' class 2-6-4Ts. The latter were to have been the last engines constructed, but the outbreak of World War 2 caused building to be resumed. Some 'Q1' class 0-6-0s and 14 LMS Stanier 2-8-0s were assembled, with War Department 2-8-0s being prepared for shipment overseas. No complete engines were built following nationalisation, although the frames, tenders and other parts for Bulleid Pacifics assembled at Brighton and Eastleigh were made at Ashford and wagon building continued on a large scale.

A list of engines arriving for repair between 26 April and 19 June 1947 gives a typical view of the variety of work undertaken in the immediate postwar period:

'R1' class 0-6-0T: 1047.
'H' class 0-4-4T: 1193, 1309, 1503, 1540.
'C' class 0-6-0: 1257, 1277, 1573.
'O1' class 0-6-0: 1258, 1384.
'N' class 2-6-0: 1407, 1812/4/6/7, 1842.
'J' class 0-6-4T: 1595.
'D' class 4-4-0: 1750.
'D1' class 4-4-0: 1727.
'L' class 4-4-0: 1763.
'L1' class 4-4-0: 1758, 1783.
'W' class 2-6-4T: 1917.
'D3' class 0-4-4T: 2374.
'E5' class 0-6-2T: 2408, 2573.
'C2' class 0-6-0: 2435.
'E3' class 0-6-2T: 2454, 2460.
'E4' class 0-6-2T: 2473, 2485, 2491, 2499, 2514/5.
'WC' class 4-6-2: 21C126, 21C130/2.

During this time three Stirling 'F1' 4-4-0s Nos 1043, 1101 and 1183 arrived for scrap. The emphasis was clearly still on the overhaul of the former SECR survivors and the Southern types built before the war. Many former LBSCR engines were also repaired at Ashford since Brighton works was busy with the building of Bulleid light Pacifics.

The works yard in the 1950s usually contained a number of engines of types not normally associated with Ashford awaiting cutting up. Many LSWR Drummond 'T9','D15', and 'S11' 4-4-0s made the one way journey, while in the early 1960s 'Schools', 'King Arthurs' and even some 'Lord Nelsons' were scrapped here. In the early 1950s the last 'F1' No 1231 stood for a long time in the yard awaiting possible preservation before being broken up. More fortunate was 'D' No 31737, withdrawn in 1956 but then restored in 1960 to the full glory of its Wainwright livery for exhibition as part of the National Collection, first at Clapham and then at York.

In the early 1960s a few steam engines, mainly Maunsell moguls, were still being repaired and even after the official end of steam in Kent a lingering presence was maintained. The repair and building of wagons continued for over 20 years, sometimes on a contract basis. Three 'C' class, Nos 31271, 31280 and 31592 were maintained as shunters until 1965, when they were superseded by USA 0-6-0Ts Nos 30065 and 30070, displaced by diesel shunters from Southampton Docks. Final closure of the works, other than for the repair of wheels and cranes, came in the 1980s, the remaining buildings becoming a light industrial estate still watched over by the well-known 19th century clock tower at the main entrance.

Ashford running shed was moved to a site in the angle between the Canterbury and Dover lines in 1931. A typical SR concrete building of the period, it had ten roads and a slope leading to a corrugated iron coaling stage. Typical allocations were:

**1 August 1937**
'Z' class 0-8-0T: 955.
'F1' class 4-4-0: 1002, 1051.
'R1' class 0-6-0T: 1010, 1147.
'O1' class 0-6-0: 1066, 1080, 1385, 1426.
'C' class 0-6-0: 1191, 1218, 1245, 1262/8, 1272, 1583/9, 1711.
'H' class 0-4-4T: 1239, 1305/6.
'N' class 2-6-0: 1400-5, 1825
'D' class 4-4-0: 1477, 1549, 1726, 1748.
'L' class 4-4-0: 1769, 1771-7, 1781.
'D1' class 0-4-2T: 2253.
'D3' class 0-4-4T: 2363/4/5, 2380.
'R1' class 0-4-4T: 1703.
'J' class 0-6-4T: 1595-9.

**20 July 1953**
'King Arthur' 4-6-0: 30803-5.
'Z' class 0-8-0T: 30953.
'R1' class 0-6-0T: 31010, 31147, 31339.
'O1' class 0-6-0: 31048, 31065/6, 31370.
'C' class 0-6-0: 31218, 31513, 31572, 31589, 31711.
'H' class 0-4-4T: 31327, 31500, 31512, 31521/2.
'N' class 2-6-0: 31400/7.
'D' class 4-4-0: 31549, 31574.
'L' class 4-4-0: 31772/4-8.
'A1X' class 0-6-0T: 32655/9, 32670/8.
'4MT' 2-6-4T: 42069, 42073, 42094-8.

Like Tonbridge, the shed provided engines for stopping trains and secondary routes rather than main line expresses which were normally hauled by engines from London and the coastal depots. Nevertheless, its resources were regularly called upon to assist with the holiday traffic at busy weekends; for example, in 1952 an Ashford 'King Arthur' was booked for the 'Kentish Belle' on summer Saturdays although an 'N' class 2-6-0 was

sometimes used instead. Some engines had specific duties; for example the 'Z' class tank shunted over the hump in the East yard and the 'R1' class 0-6-0Ts worked on the Canterbury and Whitstable line, for which they were sub-shedded at Canterbury West, until its final closure in 1953. Likewise, the 'O1' and 'A1X' classes of the 1953 allocation were outstationed at Rolvenden for much of the time for working on the former Kent and East Sussex line. Also on Ashford's allocation for many years were the five bulky but rather obscure 'J' class 0-6-4Ts built at the end of Wainwright's reign for London suburban services. After electrification in the 1920s they found a home here before the coming of LMR 2-6-4Ts built at Brighton in the early 1950s ousted them from main line stopping trains and they were withdrawn by 1951.

Again, like Tonbridge, Ashford shed took a long time to die. With electrification most work was transferred to a new depot at Chart Leacon, west of the station, the old shed continuing to service the works shunters until 1963. Subsequently an attempt was made to revive its fortunes as the South Eastern Steam Centre and several engines were based there for a while. The venture failed and, at the time of writing, the crumbling shell of the building awaits eventual demolition.

**Folkestone**
The fortunes of Folkestone changed dramatically during the second half of the 19th century. From being a small harbour handling fish and coal traffic it became a busy cross-channel ferry port and the largest seaside resort in Kent, described as 'like an English counterpart to Le Touquet'. Two different influences brought this about - the SER's interest in using the harbour as an alternative to Dover and the enterprise of the Lords of the Manor, the Earls of Radnor, in developing the new town and resort. The two things took place quite independently and in some ways in opposition to each other but the result was a considerable volume of passenger traffic for the railway to carry during the heyday years.

Although the SER purchased Folkestone Harbour in 1843 in a very derelict state it was to prove a valuable investment, giving them their own ferry port, free of the influence of the Admiralty and the competition experienced at Dover. In the same year the first regular day ferry service to Boulogne started and in 1845 a subsidiary company (the South Eastern and Continental Steam Packet Company) was formed to operate steamers from

*Below:*
**Photographs of the Folkestone Harbour branch usually feature multiples of 'R1' class 0-6-0Ts heading passenger trains up the 1 in 30 incline to the main line, freight traffic having ceased long ago. A change from the usual scene is provided by this picture of No 31154 arriving at the junction with a horsebox special on Tuesday 12 October 1954.** *J. J. Smith*

*Left:*
**The last days of the 'R1' class at Folkestone in the late 1950s with No 31010 and another of the class in store following the successful use of the Western Region pannier tanks. No 31010 had acquired a cut down chimney and cab for working through Tyler Hill tunnel on the Canterbury and Whitstable line.** *Mike Esau*

*Below left:*
**The reign of the pannier tanks on the branch was short and they were displaced when electric multiple-units took over most of the boat trains in June 1961. On the last day of steam working, No 4601, assisted at the rear of the train, clambers up to Folkestone Junction with a Continental express consisting mainly of Maunsell stock.** *P. N. Townend*

Dover and Folkestone to Calais, Boulogne and Ostend. Improvements to the harbour were carried out, notably the construction in 1863 of a new pier into deeper water and its extension in 1885, so that a fixed timetable, not dependent on the tides, could be operated, while conditions for passengers offered much greater comfort than those at Dover. The vessels also improved steadily and by 1933 some 300,000 passengers passed through the port annually, a high proportion using rail connections to and from London.

Meanwhile, the Earls of Radnor set about exploiting the opportunities for tourist and property development, provided by the attractive environment of the cliffs above the harbour. A high class resort was created with large villas, hotels and boarding houses, all having access to the well-tended open space of the Leas. Other amenities included music and a theatre. Such development was viewed at first with little interest by the SER but in 1884 they provided a new station, at first called Cheriton Arch but then renamed Radnor Park and eventually Folkestone Central. As time went on they increasingly appreciated the resort's traffic potential and appropriate services were provided. In 1896 a new Pullman type luxury train of parlour cars designed by Harry Wainwright was started, running only between London and Folkestone, while in 1922 the Folkestone expresses were accelerated to run nonstop from Charing Cross in 80 minutes for the 70 miles, among the fastest trains in Britain at the time. It was a timing as fast as the Pacific hauled 'Man of Kent' expresses of the 1950s and faster than today's electric services, although the latter run via Maidstone East and make several intermediate stops.

A problem never overcome was that of the steeply graded branch from Folkestone Harbour to the junction, which all boat trains had to negotiate. Various proposals were made for new approaches to the harbour, notably by extending the branch from Sandling Junction to Hythe and Sandgate along the coast. This was defeated by opposition from the townspeople and Lord Radnor. Thus, for more than a century, until electrification, one of the railway sights of southern England was the heavy boat trains, for several years including the empty stock of the Golden Arrow Pullman, being heaved up the curving 1 in 30 by three or four tank engines. On these duties the Stirling 'R' class 0-6-0Ts, reboilered by Wainwright as the 'R1s', reigned supreme for 67 years. Proposals to use 'Z' class 0-8-0Ts following replacement of the original swing bridge across the harbour with a heavier steel one came to nothing, as did the trials with a Bulleid light Pacific in the 1950s. Not until the dying days of steam was an acceptable substitute for the 'R1s' found. In 1958 ex-GWR pannier tank No 9770 was tried and found successful; five more (Nos 4610/6, 4626, 4630/1) arrived early in 1959 and carried out banking duties until electrification of the branch.

The allocation of the small sub-shed at Folkestone Junction was:

**1 August 1937**
'R1' class 0-6-0T: 1107, 1127/8, 1154, 1174, 1337, 1340.

**20 July 1953**
'R1' class 0-6-0T: 31047, 31069, 31107, 31128, 31154, 31337, 31340.

## Dover

Dover is a classic case of a major seaport which came into being despite the limitations of its site because it was at the narrowest crossing point of a sea separating areas of dense population. The site of the original settlement was in the narrow Dour Valley between the Western Heights and Castle Hill. Flat land suitable for large scale development was almost non-existent and the port was therefore forced out to sea, most of the activity taking place today on reclaimed land. Two other major problems were those of exposure to violent south westerly gales sweeping up the Channel and the drifting of shingle across the mouth of the Dour.

Dover was a port in Roman times and is the only functioning survivor of the original Cinque Ports (Dover, Sandwich, Romney, Hythe and Hastings) which, in the early middle ages, supplied the King with ships and men in return for certain privileges and exemptions. Over subsequent centuries a number of small scale improvements were made but today's massive outer harbour (Fig 7) owes its origin to a recommendation made in 1845 to construct a harbour of refuge capable of handling up to 20 large naval vessels. A start was made in enclosing the bay,

*Above right:*
**The shortage of space in the older part of Dover, where the Western Heights approach very close to the sea shore, is apparent in this view of 'T9' class 4-4-0 No 312 passing Hawkesbury Street Junction with a vans train on 23 September 1938. The lines to the right of the engine lead to the Marine station and the then new train ferry berth.** *F. J. Agar*

*Right:*
**Dover Priory, the main station for the town, as rebuilt by the Southern Railway in 1932 on the site of the LCDR building dating from 1861. The goods yard, where the 'H' class is shunting, still survives as carriage and locomotive berthing sidings. It also has a deep well whose water supplies are taken to Ramsgate to be used for carriage washing during periods of drought.** *Revd A. W. V. Mace*

42

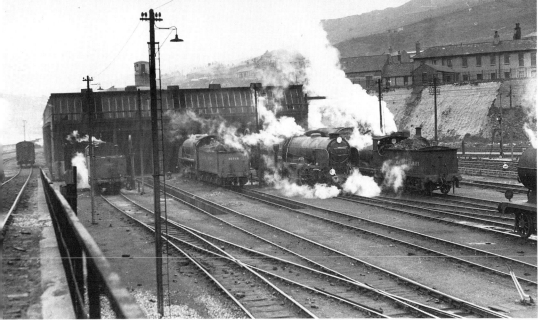

*Left:*
**Dover engine shed, a typical SR building of the 1920s, constructed to replace the older depot at Priory station. The concrete ramp on the left led to a small coaling stage. Built on reclaimed land near the sea shore, Dover shed was never an easy place at which to work because of its exposed position. Matters were even worse during World War 2 when the area was known as 'hell fire corner' because of enemy shells fired across the Channel. The engines on shed in this 1949 picture include War Department 2-8-0 No 79262 as well as more familiar Southern Railway types.** *LPC No K242/Ian Allan Ltd*

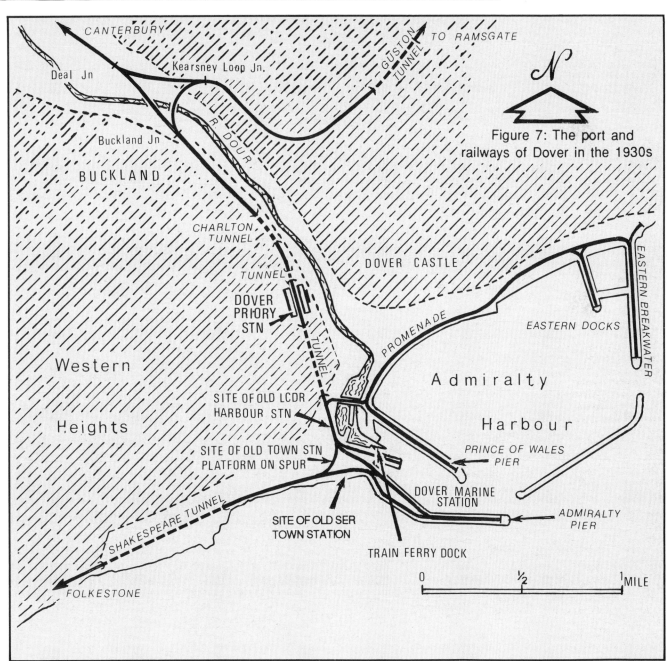

Figure 7: The port and railways of Dover in the 1930s

beginning with the south-western quarter because of its vulnerability to storms. The Admiralty Pier was begun in 1847 and by 1850 had reached 650ft from the shore, ending the menace of drifting shingle. Extension work continued until 1875 when the Admiralty, put off by the cost, lost interest in the harbour of refuge. Dover Harbour Board then decided to complete the inner harbour itself and began the Prince of Wales Pier in 1892, only for the government to decide to complete the outer harbour, which it finally did in 1909. It is within this square mile of enclosed water that subsequent development has taken place first to create the 'railway age' Western Docks and more recently to make the Eastern Docks, where most of today's road-based roll-on roll-off activity takes place.

When the railways reached Dover both the SER and the LCDR at first used stations on the side of the harbour but from 1864 the boat trains of both companies used the station which consisted of one long, narrow platform in the middle of which were slopes to quay level, on the Admiralty Pier. The ferries tied up on the leeward side and the ordeal for the passengers, transshipping at this spartan station on a wild winter day, with storm force winds and waves crashing over the pier, is not difficult to imagine. Nevertheless, this is what cross channel passengers had to endure for over 50 years, although conditions for those transferring to the liners bound for South America and West Africa which also used the port were rather better since they used a station on the less exposed Prince of Wales Pier.

Relief for ferry passengers did not come until after World War 1, use by boat trains of the splendid new Dover Marine station beginning in January 1920. Built on reclaimed land on the leeward side of the Admiralty Pier it was ready for use when the war started, and during those years fulfilled a valuable role handling ambulance trains. Appropriately, the SECR's war memorial to its 556 employees who died in the Great War (and the 626 Southern Railway employees who died on active service between 1939 and 1945) is situated at this station, which was so much in the front line of the war years.

With its stone frontage and two long island platforms beneath a high all-over roof, Dover Marine was a worthy station to handle the 'Night Ferry', the Pullman boat trains and the Royal and other VIP specials of the heyday years. Even today, its importance much reduced by the transfer of most sailings to the Eastern Docks, it remains an impressive station. Platforms 3 to 6 are under cover, roads numbers 1 and 2 being the former quayside tracks while numbers 7 and 8 were formerly used for empty stock and light engine movements. They now provide access to the new train ferry terminal opened in 1988. In steam days the empty stock of arriving boat trains was drawn out either by the train engine or a pilot on to the Admiralty Pier extension and then backed into sidings at the seaward end of the station. Similarly, empty coaches for up trains were backed from these sidings into the station, saving movements across the points and curves at the landward approaches.

Cross-channel traffic fluctuated considerably in the interwar years. Although given a stimulus by improved services, there was a general decline between 1925 and 1935 and in 1930 a decision was taken at Westminster not to proceed with a Channel

Tunnel. Instead the Southern Railway decided on the development of a ferry by which both sleeping cars and freight vehicles could be shipped to Dunkirk, necessitating the construction of a special enclosed dock at Dover because of the 22ft tidal range. Because of the need for a speedy transfer of sleeping cars to the ferry on arrival from London the dock had to be near as possible to the Marine station. It was built in line with the main harbour entrance, creating both construction and operating problems when high waves entered the harbour in winter. Construction was eventually completed in 1936 and, apart from the war years, it continued in use for passenger traffic until the 'Night Ferry' sleeping car service ceased to run in 1980 and for freight until the new train ferry terminal was opened.

After the opening of the Marine station the main Dover engine shed was moved in 1928 from the Priory station to a site on the sea shore parallel to the main line just outside the new station. Its concrete building, typical of several built by the Southern

at this time, housed six roads; a concrete ramp led up to a small coaling stage, the turntables being at the station end of the site. Typical allocations were:

**1 August 1937**
'King Arthur' 4-6-0: 770/1.
'P' class 0-6-0T: 1027, 1178, 1323, 1325, 1555-8.
'O1' class 0-6-0: 1065, 1108, 1378, 1390.
'C' class 0-6-0: 1720/1/2.
'H' class 0-4-4T: 1259, 1261/3/5/9, 1307, 1521, 1530/1/2.
'D1' class 4-4-0: 1145, 1246, 1470, 1487, 1545, 1727, 1749.
'L1' class 4-4-0: 1753-9.
'N' class 2-6-0: 1865/6/7.
'E2' class 0-6-0T: 2106/7.

**20 July 1953**
'King Arthur' 4-6-0: 30775/6/7, 30796/7/8.

*Above left:*
**Life at Dover shed revolved around duties connected with the boat trains and 'L' class 4-4-0 No 1778 is seen here shunting empty stock on the Admiralty Pier on a fine summer evening. The coach is one of the matchboard brakes designed in the early 1920s by Richard Maunsell for use on boat trains.**
*P. Ransome Wallis collection, National Railway Museum, York*

*Left:*
**Several of the ports of Southern England had quayside lines where only small shunting engines were allowed. Dover was no exception and the shed usually had an allocation of engines for working to sidings at the Eastern Docks. In the 1950s the shunters included ex LSWR 'B4' class 0-4-0T No 30084, seen on Dover promenade on Monday 2 July 1956. Sometimes these trips were preceded by a pilotman carrying a red flag.**
*John Head*

45

'Schools' 4-4-0: 30918/9, 30920/1/3.
'P' class 0-6-0T: 31027, 31178, 31323.
'B4' class 0-4-0T: 30084.
'Z' class 0-8-0T: 30952.
'C' class 0-6-0: 31113, 31150, 31191, 31243, 31317.
'O1' class 0-6-0: 31258, 31425, 31430/4.
'H' class 0-4-4T: 31278, 31328/9, 31531.
'R1' class 0-4-4T: 31661 (in store)
'D1' class 4-4-0: 31145, 31246/7, 31470.
'L1' class 4-4-0: 31753/4/5.
'E2' class 0-6-0T: 32108/9.
'Battle of Britain' 4-6-2: 34072/3/4.
'Merchant Navy' 4-6-2: 35029/30.
'4MT' 2-6-4T: 42074-9.
'E5' class 0-6-2T: 32593 (stationary boiler).

The work at Dover shed was heavily geared to boat train traffic, the 1953 allocation reflecting its postwar growth. Whereas in prewar days the largest boat train engines, the 'Lord Nelsons', were allocated to Stewarts Lane and Dover used double headed 4-4-0s for its main duty on the 'Night Ferry', by the 1950s the shed had its own Pacifics for the heaviest trains. The 'King Arthurs' were mainly used for relief and other boat trains, the 'Schools' only rarely being used on them although they often worked one of Dover's main domestic turns, the 4.15pm 'Man of Kent' from Charing Cross. The 4-4-0s and 'H' class undertook most of the local duties, including assisting main line trains up the steep gradients of the Deal line, while the moguls were available for ferry wagon and other freight trains. Shunting work around the docks was always important, only the smallest 'B4' and 'P' class tanks being allowed to work along the quay lines to the Eastern Docks, where there were at that time various factories and an oil storage depot.

Life at Dover shed bred a hardy race of enginemen. In such an exposed position on the sea front jobs like clearing ashes from smokeboxes in a winter gale could be horrific, while shunting carriages in the sidings on the end of the Admiralty Pier, with nothing more than the meagre cab of a 'C' class 0-6-0 for protection from the waves crashing over the breakwater, was a working environment few would tolerate today. The shed closed in 1961. It was demolished to make way for an extension to Dover Town goods yard and today no trace remains of its once busy existence.

## Ramsgate

Unlike most major railway centres, Ramsgate has always been of much greater importance for passenger traffic than for freight, deriving its significance not only from the great volume of summer holiday and excursion traffic to Thanet but also from the fact that, following rationalisation of railways in the area in the 1920s, the major servicing facilities were concentrated there. A completely new station was built, unfortunately at some distance both from the sea and the old town centre. Barn like in appearance, with high arched windows, the main building gives access to two long curving island platforms at which trains can arrive or depart for London from opposite directions. A long covered carriage shed was also in due course provided, with a locomotive shed and a goods depot beyond. A mechanical carriage washing plant was built at the eastern end of the layout in 1957.

With these facilities Ramsgate played a major part in providing engines and stock for regular Kent coast domestic services for the last three decades or so of steam operation. Locomotive duties were generally shared with Stewarts Lane and Bricklayer's Arms. It also catered for local trains and serviced the stock of many day excursions during their stay at the coast. The engine shed, opened in 1930, was another of the Southern's concrete structures with six roads, a spacious yard and a coaling plant. A feature of the yard for many years was an unrebuilt Stirling 'O' class No A98. Fitted with a long extension to its chimney, it did duty as a stationary boiler; in 1953 it was replaced by 'D' class No

*Above:*

**Ramsgate as rebuilt by the Southern Railway in the 1920s. The huge brick station building on the right, with its lofty booking hall survives today, as do the carriage and engine sheds as part of the depot for electric multiple units. In this scene from Monday 6 April 1953, 'Schools' No 30915 *Brighton* departs with one of the 'rounders' from Victoria on its way back to London Charing Cross via Dover and Ashford.** *R. C. Riley*

31501, sadly fallen from grace with a pair of driving wheels removed. Typical allocations were:

### February 1946
'Schools' 4-4-0: 909-23.
'C' class 0-6-0: 1004, 1592.
'H' class 0-4-4T: 1016, 1164, 1182, 1521/2/3.
'O1' class 0-6-0: 1080, 1316.
'F1' class 4-4-0: 1151.
'B1' class 4-4-0: 1451/2.
'L' class 4-4-0: 1778-81.

### 20 July 1953
'Schools' 4-4-0: 30911-4/6/7, 30922.
'C' class 0-6-0: 31004, 31245, 31252, 31271, 31298, 31592.
'H' class 0-4-4T: 31276, 31324/6.
'L1' class 4-4-0: 31756/7.
'L' class 4-4-0: 31779, 31780/1.
'Battle of Britain' 4-6-2: 34075-86, 34096-9, 34100.
'4MT' 2-6-4T: 42067/8, 42070/1/2.

Apart from a few 0-6-0s for local goods and shunting work, the allocation was dominated by passenger engines. The 'Schools' worked mainly on business trains to London in the prewar era, being replaced by light Pacifics after the war. Because of a shortage of maintenance staff at Ramsgate, rebuilt 'West Country' class engines replaced unrebuilt members of the class in the late 1950s.

Since they were relatively modern, Ramsgate's steam age facilities were easily adapted for use by multiple units when electrification took place in 1959. They still stand today, the railway environment of Ramsgate, apart from the trains themselves, being a rather fine time capsule of the 1920s.

## Faversham
Faversham's importance as a railway centre derived from three factors — its functions as an industrial town, a pre-railway age port and, after 1860, a junction for the lines to Thanet and Dover. The port area is situated north of the town alongside Faversham

Creek, from which small vessels have access to the Swale and the Thames estuary. The safeguarding of the town's position as a port was one of the reasons given for the building of the East Kent Railway and the branch to the creek was opened in 1860, two years after the main line.

Curving away from the Thanet line east of the station it served the town's coal yard, a goods depot and a meat factory before reaching a six-road yard where wagons were sorted before going to the various factories and sidings alongside Standard Quay. A great variety of goods traffic was handled and fed to and from the main line. It included jam, cement, coal, animal feeds and the products of the town's three major industries — brewing, bricks and munitions. Faversham was thus a microcosm of the situation regarding railway goods traffic in Kent, where the majority of trains conveyed a mixture of general freight rather than the trainloads of a single commodity common elsewhere.

For a century the Faversham Creek branch lived a busy life, serving the needs of the local economy. A small engine such as a Brighton 'Terrier' was sometimes used for shunting on the quay, but 4-4-0s and 'C' and 'O1' class 0-6-0s were also permitted; one of the latter distinguished itself by falling headlong into the creek, requiring the services of a breakdown crane to retrieve it. But by the end of the steam age road transport was making serious inroads into railway general freight and by the mid-1960s the lines along the quay had been closed. However, great quantities of fruit traffic, much of it imported, continued to be handled in the sidings near the station. Eventually this also succumbed and today the depot of East Kent Packers, the town's largest fruit handling enterprise, covers the site of the former goods yard and coal depot, although the course of the creek branch is still plainly visible from the vicinity of the station.

Although disused and trackless, part of Faversham steam shed, a listed building, still stands in the angle between the Thanet and Dover lines, east of the station. The remaining part is the extension added on the north side to an earlier two-road shed built in 1860. Typical allocations were:

**1 August 1937**
'B1' class 4-4-0: 1021, 1452.
'F1' class 4-4-0: 1217.
'D1' class 4-4-0: 1247, 1502/5/9, 1739.
'C' class 0-6-0: 1090, 1150, 1221, 1234, 1242, 1260, 1271, 1461, 1589, 1592, 1572, 1584.
'O1' class 0-6-0: 1106, 1369, 1379, 1430.
'R' class 0-4-4T: 1667, 1673/4.

**20 July 1953**
'E' class 4-4-0: 31166.
'D1' class 4-4-0: 31487/9, 31492/4, 31505.
'C' class 0-6-0: 31253/5/6, 31267/8, 31461, 31481, 31714/5.
'H' class 0-4-4T: 31305, 31503.
'U' class 2-6-0: 31637, 31803/4/6.
'N' class 2-6-0: 31850/2/4.
'2MT' 2-6-2T: 41308-12.

The 30 engines consisted of 4-4-0s and 0-4-4Ts for local passenger trains and 0-6-0s and 2-6-0s for local and longer distance freight. The moguls, along with the 'Schools' class, were the largest engines able to be turned on the shed's hand operated table. In the last days of steam, modernisation arrived in the form of the LMR Ivatt 2-6-2Ts to replace pre-grouping engines on local services such as the Sheerness branch.

The shed closed to steam on completion of Phase 1 of the Kent coast electrification project in 1959 but it remained as a 'garage' for diesel locomotives until its use finally faded away due to declining traffic some 20 years later.

*Below:*
**A view from the footbridge east of Faversham station on Friday 12 July 1957 featuring a down Thanet express headed by No 34067 *Tangmere*. The Dover line is on the left behind the locomotives parked outside the shed, whilst ferry wagons and agricultural traffic are in evidence in the sidings. The branch to Faversham Creek left the main line on the extreme right of the picture.** *P. J. Lynch*

# Chapter 4

# The Continental expresses

In 1991 Dover ranked as Britain's busiest ferry port, handling 15.9 million passengers and over 12 million tons of cargo, most of it by the roll-on, roll-off ferries which make at least 30 crossings a day in each direction, mainly to Calais or Boulogne. The centre of activity is in the road-oriented Eastern Docks, where since the 1950s and at an increasing pace in the 1980s many millions of pounds have been invested in facilities for the trans-shipment of cars, coaches, lorries and trailers. During this time the rail-served Western Docks have become the neglected corner of the port, the only substantial investment being the £8.9m spent on the new train ferry berth on the Admiralty Pier. Dover Western Docks, as the former Marine station is now called, is for much of the time a strangely silent and deserted place where stopping and semi-fast services from Victoria via Chatham reverse. The ever-declining number of traditional foot passengers, even those travelling on the luxury VSOE Pullman, have to endure a bus journey to board the vehicle ferries in the Eastern Docks. Rail passengers are treated very much as the poor relations of the millions who pass through by car and coach.

**Between the wars.**
The situation is a far cry from the days in the 1920s and the 1930s when the SR and the Nord Railway of France, along with the Pullman Car Company and the Compagnie Internationale des Wagons-Lits, sought to develop faster and more luxurious rail and ferry services through the port. Before World War 1, continental traffic had been of great importance to the SECR and had been handled at several different locations, including Gravesend, Port Victoria on the Isle of Grain and Queenborough (Sheerness) on the Isle of Sheppey. The last two were a legacy of pre-1899 competition and had nearly ceased to be concerned with continental operations by the 1920s. On the other hand the Admiralty decided at this time that under peacetime conditions Dover was no longer required as an operational base. Thus, with the new Marine station available for civilian traffic after relinquishing its wartime role, the scene was all set to develop the port as a major terminal for the short sea routes, with Folkestone playing an important but subsidiary role.

An increase in traffic would clearly require longer and heavier trains pulled by larger locomotives. The SR therefore set about a programme of improvements, mainly by bridge strengthening, on the routes to the ports. Having decided upon Victoria

*Below:*
**A Continental express of the 1930s leaves Dover Marine for Victoria headed by 'Lord Nelson' No 854 *Howard of Effingham*, a type built with the needs of the boat trains in mind. The coaching stock consists entirely of corridor vehicles, the first carriage being one of the matchboard brakes with end windows and many Pullman features.**
*By courtesy of the National Railway Museum, York*

*Top:*
**The prewar 'Night Ferry' passing Bromley South on 18 October 1936 behind 'L1' class No 1758 and 'L' class No 1764, a few days after the train's introduction. Mail vans were always at the front end of the train on arrival at Victoria, with sleeping cars, catering vehicles and accommodation for seated passengers behind. This was a heavy train, each sleeping car weighing 55 tons, and it proved beyond the capabilities of the 'Lord Nelsons' to keep time with it. Double-headed 4-4-0s were therefore always provided in the 1930s.** *H. C. Casserley*

*Above:*
**Early post-war days at Folkestone Junction. A work stained 'King Arthur' No 763 *Sir Bors de Ganis* waits in the boat train sidings while another of the class leaves for Victoria. The rapid production of the Bulleid light Pacifics from 1946 onwards meant that the 'Arthurs' were soon displaced from regular boat train duties.** *Revd A. C. Cawston*

rather than, as in prewar days, Charing Cross as the main London terminal for boat trains, priority was given to improvements on the Victoria-Bickley-Orpington-Tonbridge route to Dover, on which 21 bridges were rebuilt by July 1925. This made possible the use of the 'King Arthur' class, weighing a little over 80 tons in place of the 53 ton 4-4-0s used earlier, Nos 763-772 being the 'Arthurs' originally allocated to the continental services. By 1926 the Catford loop and the Swanley to Ashford via Maidstone East line had also been upgraded as relief boat train routes, the process

being completed with the rebuilding of bridges on the former LCDR line via Chatham and Canterbury in 1927. In all, over 100 bridges were reconstructed for heavier weights during a three year period, giving the operators a higher degree of flexibility in the routing of boat trains. The way was also prepared for the introduction of the 83 ton 'Lord Nelson' class, the Southern's biggest 4-6-0s, and the 'Merchant Navy' Pacifics after World War 2, both originally being designed with the needs of continental traffic in mind.

Equally revolutionary was the change in the coaching stock used on the boat trains. The use of Pullman cars, which had operated on the SECR since 1910, in a livery of crimson lined with gold and with white roofs, was increased in the early 1920s. Most prewar rolling stock had been non-corridor and, in order to improve the standard of accommodation and to provide vehicles suitable to run with Pullmans, Richard Maunsell gave priority in his early designs to improved coaches for the boat trains. The earliest, which became known as matchboard stock from the distinctive body sides below the waistline, displayed several Pullman features, including gangways and inward opening doors to the end vestibules. The third class compartments seated only three per side due to their restricted 8ft 6in width, but this allowed an unusually wide corridor, ideal for boat trains. The underframe and bogies were of a new design which remained basically unchanged until the end of the SR's history.

Through the late 1920s and the early 1930s Maunsell produced a range of standard coach designs. The vehicles, which were built in considerable numbers, were of a similar basic construction with steel panelled, timber framed bodies on steel underframes. A very distinct design for the boat trains was the 'Nondescript' brakes, produced in 1933. Internally they were saloons fitted out to a high degree of comfort but not given a class; they could therefore be labelled for first, second or third class use as traffic demanded. The accommodation was split into three saloons, each with doors to the outside and an off-centre gangway. Several 'Nondescripts' survive in preservation on the Bluebell and Kent and East Sussex Railways; on the latter they form part of the dining car train, giving passengers ample time to appreciate the comfort of SR 1930s boat train travel.

In addition to its railway improvements the company invested in new ships, much more luxuriously appointed than those used earlier, for the short sea routes. They included the *Isle of Thanet* and the *Maid of Kent*, delivered in 1925; at 2,700 tons and capable of 21 knots they were then the Southern's largest ships. In 1929 came the larger and even more luxurious *Canterbury* built exclusively to carry 'Golden Arrow' passengers. The vessels operated alongside the French-owned *Cote d'Azur* and

*Above:*
**The dawn of the postwar heyday of the 'Golden Arrow'. New 'West Country' Pacific No 21C119, later *Bideford,* attracts an admiring audience as its waits to leave Victoria in the spring of 1946. The first runs of the restored train had 'Merchant Navy' No 21C1 *Channel Packet* in charge, but this locomotive soon returned to Exeter, leaving light Pacifics as the usual engines.** *C. R. L. Coles*

*Below:*
**The restoration of the 'Golden Arrow' brought the return to its peacetime role of the *Canterbury,* the ship built by the Southern Railway in the 1920s especially for this service. This view of the gracious dining room taken in 1946 shows that, for some people at least, life was returning to normal after years of austerity.** *By courtesy of the National Railway Museum, York*

*Cote d'Argent* and the Belgian *Prince Leopold* and *Prince Baudouin.*

Later, for the construction of the first British passenger train ferry, to operate between Dover and Dunkirk, Sir Herbert Walker sought the advice of the Department of Naval Architecture at Newcastle University and it is not therefore surprising that the three coal fired ships built for the service, the *Twickenham Ferry,* the *Hampton Ferry* and the *Shepperton Ferry* were constructed on the Tyne rather than the Clyde, as were other SR ships. They were delivered in 1934 and 1935 and remained the mainstay of the 'Night Ferry' until 1969, when the *Hampton Ferry* was the first to be taken off. Two tracks across the linkspans at the ports led to the stern of the vessels. On the train ferry deck there were four tracks, the sleeping cars using those in the centre and the ferry wagons the outer spaces. Two platforms were provided from which passengers could gain access to the saloon and dining facilities on the upper decks. On day sailings the ships could take up to 40 ferry wagons, although in later years an increased proportion of the space was taken up with road vehicles.

Thus the Southern invested heavily in the cross Channel services, although the depressed economic conditions of the early 1930s meant that passenger traffic actually fell by about 25% compared with the early 1920s. However, most of the equipment showed its worth when the war came. To those accustomed to the situation today where frequent ferries shuttle back and forth across the Channel, the infrequency of the service in those days is quite remarkable for the arrival of a steamer at Dover or Folkestone always seemed something of an event. In 1928 the basic service consisted of three boat trains from Victoria each day for ferries from Dover to Calais, three for the Dover-Ostend service and two for that between Folkestone and Boulogne. The pattern was similar in July 1938, with morning departures from Victoria at 9.00am for Paris via Folkestone and Boulogne, 10.30am for Paris and Ostend via Dover and 11.00am with first and second class passengers only, for Paris via Dover and Calais. The three afternoon departures, at 2.00pm, 3.00pm and 4.30pm served Paris via

**Restoration of the 'Night Ferry' service came later and it was not until 15 December 1947 that the first postwar train ran with No 21C156 *Croydon* piloting 'L1' 4-4-0 No 1757. As the length and weight of the train increased, double-heading remained common, sometimes with two light Pacifics.** *R. C. Riley Collection*

**The proud days of the all-Pullman 'Golden Arrow' in the early 1950s, with 'Britannia' No 70004 *William Shakespeare* in charge of the 5.55pm up train in Folkestone Warren on Thursday 15 May 1952.** *J. J. Smith*

*Right:*
**Another memory of the heyday years of the 'Golden Arrow'. Dressed with the full regalia of headboard, arrows, Union and Tricolour flags, No 70004 *William Shakespeare* was portrayed alongside a diminutive 'P' class 0-6-0T, No 31558, beneath the coaling plant at Stewarts Lane shed. The engine had been cleaned to perfection, and Mr Hardy, the shedmaster, only allowed it to be photographed in this position for a few moments.**
*John Ashman*
*FRPS/Courtesy Mike Esau*

*Below right:*
**Early in 1954, 1,750 hp diesel-electric No 10202 was tried on a daily diagram involving both the up and down 'Night Ferry' and the 'Golden Arrow' — an increase in productivity compared with steam, but a miserable substitute aesthetically. Fortunately the experiment lasted for only a short time and, apart from trials with sister locomotive No 10203 a year later, steam soon returned to both duties.** *Ian Allan Library*

Dover and Calais, Ostend via Dover and Paris via Folkestone and Boulogne respectively. By this time an additional service was provided by the 'Night Ferry', leaving at 10.00pm. In the up direction most services reached Victoria in the late afternoon or early evening, the exception being the 11pm late evening arrival from Paris via Folkestone and Boulogne and the 'Night Ferry' due at 9.10am. All of these services were of course, supplemented by the running of relief trains at holiday times.

**The 'Golden Arrow'**
Born of Sir Herbert Walker's dream of providing a luxury service from Victoria to match those being developed on the continent, the Golden Arrow had rather a long gestation period in the 1920s. The Southern introduced an all-Pullman boat train in 1924. It became known as the 'White Pullman' and made connection at Calais with both the 'Fleche d'Or' Pullman train for Paris and the 'Cote d'Azur' bound for the Riviera. The full all first class 'Golden Arrow' service, with separate customs examination at Dover and a specially allocated ship, did not, however begin until 15 May 1929. It left Victoria at 11.00am with a timing of 95 minutes to Dover; the *Canterbury* sailed at 12.55pm on a schedule of 50-55 minutes and the connecting train for Paris left Calais at 2.25pm to reach the Gare du Nord at 5.35pm. The up train left Paris at 12.00, the steamer connection reaching Dover at 4.40pm. The London train left only 17 minutes later and, on a 98 minute schedule, reached Victoria at 6.35pm.

Unfortunately, the introduction of the 'Golden Arrow' coincided with the slump of the early 1930s and a consequent decline in the demand for luxury train travel, so that by 1932 second class vehicles had been added to the train. Another change occurred in 1935, when the northbound service was routed via Boulogne and Folkestone so that one set of cars could work the

train both ways in France. The timing of the down train was little affected, but the up service now left Paris at 10.30am, crossed the Channel between 1.50pm and 3.20pm and reached Victoria at 5.30pm. One effect of this was that the *Canterbury* could work only one leg of the 'Golden Arrow' on any one day. By the late 1930s the train consisted mainly of ordinary stock supplemented by three or four first class Pullmans; it ceased to run from 3 September 1939, when the outbreak of war brought the closure of Dover to civilian traffic.

### The 'Night Ferry'
To operate alongside the 'Golden Arrow' the SR introduced the 'Night Ferry' service in 1936. It enabled its passengers, mainly diplomats, businessmen and the wealthy on their way to join the great European Trains de Luxe to occupy their sleeping berths in the middle or late evening, cross the Channel in the early hours

and reach the Gare du Nord around the civilised hour of 9.00am. The down train was a somewhat elusive one, seen only at Victoria or at a suburban or country station in Kent as it slipped through in the hours before midnight. The up train, however, with the sleeping cars in their dark blue livery with yellow lining and bronze CIWL crests became a distinctive sight to early morning travellers on the Tonbridge route from Dover to London which it generally used.

For this service, all steel sleeping cars, known as the F (for ferry) type were built to the British loading gauge. Twelve numbered 3788 to 3799 entered service in 1936. Weighing nearly 55 tons they were identical in layout, with nine compartments each containing an upper and lower berth, the upper berth being folded back when the compartment was used for single occupancy. Full details of the layout and features of the cars are given by Behrend and Buchanan (*Night Ferry*, 1985) or can be seen in

*Above:*
**The time honoured picture of Folkestone Harbour, with 'R1s' Nos 31047, 31337 and 31340 having just crossed the swing bridge at the entrance to the inner harbour in August 1952. Weight restrictions here accounted for the 67 year reign of these locomotives on the branch. Many of the buildings behind the train disappeared when the port was altered to handle vehicle ferries in the late 1960s and the scene makes an interesting contrast with that today (Chapter 11).** *P. J. Lynch*

the examples preserved at the National Railway Museum (No 3792) or at the Bluebell Railway (No 3801, of a later postwar series).

At Victoria the train used platform 2, adjacent to which was a customs examination and passport control room. The formation of the departing train from front to rear was usually coaches for seated passengers, catering vehicles, sleeping cars and mail vans. Catering was provided in two Pullman cars, one a 12-wheeler providing suppers for sleeping car occupants and the other a third class vehicle for other passengers. The corridor between them was kept locked to prevent the mingling of those who had already passed through customs and passport control and the seated passengers who had not. The latter gained access to their accommodation at Victoria via platform 1. Behind the sleeping cars and bringing up the rear would be two or three four-wheeled vans for the carriage of mail and registered baggage. They were mainly from among a series of French built all steel vehicles dating from 1928/9; the earliest built had a guard's compartment and remained in use until the end of the train's life. The Southern had also, in 1935, built three four-wheeled vans especially for the train; with a central guard's roof lookout above the general roof line, they were of very distinctive appearance.

The train was brought into Victoria from Pimlico carriage sidings an hour or so before its advertised 10pm departure time, the 'E2' 0-6-0T or 0-4-4T empty stock pilot uncoupling but remaining at the rear of the train to provide assistance up to Grosvenor Bridge. Through Kent the train was booked to travel via Tonbridge but in fact might use any of the main boat train routes. On arrival at Dover Marine just before midnight the vans and sleepers were uncoupled and drawn out by the pilot, usually a 'C' class 0-6-0 or an 'E2'. At Hawkesbury Street Junction it reversed and propelled the vehicles down the special lines to the linkspan, a double shunt being needed to position the vans and

sleepers aboard the ship. When shunting was completed the sleeping cars were jacked up to take the weight off their springs and locked to the train deck by chains with screw couplings. When this was all completed the ferry sailed at 12.35am, reaching Dunkirk at 4.30am.; after more shunting the train left for Paris at 5.10am.

From its inauguration on 14 October 1936 the service ran into problems, mainly concerned with gales in the Channel and docking at Dover, which plagued it throughout its existence. It was also too heavy to be handled by a 'Lord Nelson', the staple motive power for boat trains in the 1930s; with double-heading using 4-6-0s banned because of weight restrictions, the use of pairs of 4-4-0s, usually 'D1s', 'E1s' and 'L1s' from Dover shed, became the norm. The service lasted for less than three years before it was suspended for the duration of the war, all the sleeping vehicles being returned to France before some were acquired in 1942 for work in Germany. A full flowering of the 'Night Ferry' had to wait until the 1950s, when the availability of more coaches and larger engines to pull them made it possible for a greater range of destinations to be served.

### The postwar years

By the spring of 1946 regular Continental Expresses again became a feature of the Kent main lines, three leaving Victoria

each morning. The first, at 9.00am was for Dover and the ferry to Ostend and the second, at 9.20am for Dover and Calais. The 'Golden Arrow', which resumed on 15 April, followed at 10.00am.

The ordinary boat trains were at first worked by 'King Arthurs', the 'Lord Nelsons' having by this time been transferred to the Bournemouth line, but the duties were quickly taken over by the new Bulleid Pacifics which were emerging from Eastleigh and Brighton works. They worked the 'Golden Arrow' from the outset, No.21C1 *Channel Packet* being especially brought from Exmouth Junction; newly painted in green, it worked the 'Arrow' for the first two weeks of its revival. On a trial trip on 13 April, hauling nine coaches, a speed of 78mph was attained near Paddock Wood, but the regular train was allowed 100 minutes, five more than prewar, for the Victoria-Dover journey. Platform 8 at Victoria became the regular arrival and departure platform, the down train leaving at 10.00am giving an arrival time in Paris of 6.45pm. The northbound train left at 11.35am and the British Pullman reached Victoria at 8.30pm.

The formation of the train in these early postwar years was eight or nine Pullmans plus two vans (around 390 tons), a bar car being an innovation compared with the prewar train. Motive power was usually provided by a light Bulleid Pacific, the train having certain regular engines, for example Nos 21C119 and 21C157. Sometimes a 'Merchant Navy' was used, but those on the Eastern section were mainly allocated to Dover for the heavier 'Night Ferry', the 'Arrow' being a regular Stewarts Lane duty.

The early 1950s were without doubt the heyday years of the 'Golden Arrow' and the 'Night Ferry'. On 11 June 1951 a magnificent set of new 1st class Pullmans built by the Birmingham Railway Carriage and Wagon Company made its debut on the former. They were named *Cygnus, Perseus, Hercules, Pegasus, Aquila, Orion* and *Carina*, while three older cars (*Minerva*, par-

lour second No 35 and parlour brake second No 208) were rebuilt to match. The train had a seating capacity of 262, comprising 184 first and 78 second class places. The showpiece engine at the Festival of Britain exhibition, No 70004 *William Shakespeare*, was put on the train on leaving the show and became for a while the regular engine, along with No 70014 *Iron Duke*.

In 1952 Mr Richard Hardy became shedmaster at Stewarts Lane and the standard of presentation of some of the engines in his care became a legend. By this time the down train had been diverted to run to Folkestone, leaving Victoria at 1pm (2pm in summer) and the magnificent all Pullman train set out behind an engine that reflected hours of work by the cleaning gang. With polished buffers, frame ends and smokebox hinges and brass, copper and cab fittings gleaming the engine was a sight to behold in the sombre world of postwar Britain. All across south London and Kent householders stood in their gardens and bystanders on bridges to watch the 'Golden Arrow' go through each day.

These vintage years of the famous train were to be short lived. The speed and increasing reliability of air travel began to eat into the market for which the 'Golden Arrow' catered and the number of passengers using it decreased. As in prewar years, a process of gradual decline set in, with ordinary coaches beginning to replace the Pullmans as early as the mid-1950s. Rebuilt Bulleid Pacifics became the regular motive power after the transfer away of the 'Britannias' and it fell to No 34100 *Appledore* to work the last steam turn on 11 June 1961. The train itself continued to run behind an electric locomotive until September 1972, by which

*Above:*
**'Schools' class locomotives were never common on boat trains despite the fact that the whole class was allocated to the South Eastern Division of the Southern Region in the 1950s. This photograph of No 30921 *Shrewsbury*, climbing out of Dover towards Lydden in the last year of steam working, is therefore a relatively rare one.** *Gerald Siviour*

*Above right:*
**No set of photographs of Continental expresses would be complete without some indication of what travellers found on the other side of the Channel. In this picture a boat train from Paris, headed by a PLM Pacific No 231K4, sedately traverses Boulogne Quay in 1965 viewed in wonderment by a party of English schoolboys.** *P. J. Lynch*

time only four Pullmans, by now nameless and in blue and grey livery, were included in the formation.

Resumption of the 'Night Ferry' came later than the 'Golden Arrow', partly because of wartime losses of rolling stock. Thus only four sleeping cars were in the first train from Paris on 14 December 1947. The situation steadily improved and by 1952 new building had made 20 cars available, up to nine running in any one train. Because of the overnight journey and the morning arrival in time for meetings, the train maintained its popularity with businessmen and diplomats for some time after the appeal of the 'Golden Arrow' began to decline. Its popularity was enhanced in June 1957 by the introduction of a through coach to Brussels, running between Dunkirk and Lille in the Basle express and thence in a Belgian local train. Ten years later the train acquired its own through sleeping car to Basle, ostensibly for the use of winter skiers, although the lack of a through baggage car or sufficient room in the cabins for skis was a distinct disadvantage. The service lasted for only two seasons!

Although many Bulleid Pacifics were available by the time the 'Night Ferry' resumed, they did not end the need for double heading, the first down service being worked by No 21C156 *Croydon* piloting by 'L1' No 1757. 'Merchant Navies' were capable of working the train unaided and frequently did so in the early 1950s when various members of the class were allocated to Dover, whose No 430 duty covered the up and down 'Night Ferry' and a daytime boat train. Light Pacifics could also work the train unaided, but were prone to slipping and liable to run short of water so that a pilot was often provided. This would sometimes be another light Pacific, especially on Saturdays from about 1956, but the 4-4-0s of Classes D1, E1 or L1 were often used, the smaller engine sometimes being coupled inside the Pacific. 'Britannias' also made a few appearances, particularly in May 1953 when No 70030 *Thomas Hardy* was one of a number

on loan to the SR to replace temporarily withdrawn Bulleid Pacifics (Chapter 10). The only intrusions on steam's domination until the Kent Coast electrification came in the spring of 1954 and 1955, when diesel electric locomotives Nos 10202 and 10203 respectively underwent trials for a week or so.

Apart from its increased weight, a number of other changes were made to the postwar 'Night Ferry' compared with the situation before 1939. The Pullmans providing the catering were replaced with a Maunsell SR twinset restaurant and kitchen car. From 20 September 1954 the up train was routed on weekdays via Chatham due to its Tonbridge route path being required for a Tunbridge Wells-Charing Cross commuter train on Mondays to Fridays and an Ashford-London train on Saturdays. From 10 April 1955 the up train ran again via Tonbridge on Sunday mornings. The Victoria arrival remained constant at 9.10am, although departure and arrival times in Paris varied a great deal over the years.

The first appearance of an electric locomotive on the 'Night Ferry' took place on 8 June 1959 when No 5003 worked the down service. But the association of steam with the train did not finally end until 1 January 1962, several months after the official end of main line steam in Kent. On a day of disruption caused by heavy snow and icing of the third rail the up train appeared behind Nos 34100 *Appledore* and 'N' class 2-6-0 31412, cheered on its way by passengers waiting on wayside stations for stranded electric trains!

The train outlived the steam age by nearly 20 years. Even in the early 1970s eight sleeping cars ran regularly, the seating passengers being conveyed by electric multiple-units. But increasing air competition, the ending in 1976 of the contract between BR and Wagons Lits and the increasing age of the rolling stock all meant that its days were coming to an end. In December 1977 the last of the '71' class electric locomotives was withdrawn and from then on it was usually worked by a '33' class diesel or a '73' class electro-diesel. The handling of cross-Channel freight by road trailers became ever more profitable, while the economics of the passenger operation worsened. The inevitable happened on 31 October 1980 when No 33043, adorned with a London-Paris-Brussels 'Night Ferry' circular headboard similar to that carried in the late 1950s, pulled out of Victoria with the final down working consisting of five cars bound for Paris and two for Brussels. The up train was worked by No 73142, the cars returning empty to Paris the following evening. Thus ended the first era of through sleeping cars between Britain and mainland Europe; their revival awaits the opening of the Channel Tunnel.

Although vehicle carrying services had operated from Dover since the 1930s and a specialist car ferry terminal opened in the Eastern Docks as early as 1953, the bulk of the continental traffic in the 1950s still consisted of foot passengers who made their way to and from the ports by rail. As late as 1958 only four small car carrying ferries operated out of Dover. The year-round pattern of rail services was between six and eight Continental Expresses daily to and from Victoria. Departures from London, apart from the 'Night Ferry', were usually around mid-morning and early afternoon, with arrivals there in mid and late afternoon and mid-evening. About two-thirds of the trains were routed via Dover, with a journey time of around 92 minutes from Victoria, while the rest went via Folkestone, the journey time being just over 100 minutes because of the need for reversal at Folkestone Junction. For the regular Continental Expresses, Pacific power was the general rule.

These last years of steam saw a great increase in tourist traffic, particularly in the months between June and September and at other holiday times. Larger ferries than those used between the wars came into service (J. Hendy, *This is Dover and Folkestone*). Most of the regular boat trains needed at least one relief during the summer and around a dozen 'Q' (if required) paths were provided in the working timetables to be used when the traffic justified it. In these circumstances the availability of alternative boat train routes was invaluable, that to Ashford via Swanley and Maidstone East being the most favoured alternative to the main line via Tonbridge. Some were routed via Chatham, especially on weekdays, since the heavy holiday traffic to Thanet restricted the availability of paths at weekends. Other resources were also stretched to the limit and places like Eardley Road carriage sidings near Streatham in south London, where long rows of Maunsell coaches slumbered through the winter months, became deserted for much of the day in summer. Even after the arrival of 'Standard' class 5 4-6-0s at Stewarts Lane in 1955 the locomotive department had frequently to revert to the use of 'King Arthurs' for relief trains and the appearance of 'N1' class mogul No 31822 (on a boat train) on 13 August in that year showed just how short of suitable engines the SR could become on busy days.

By the end of the 1950s the age of the package tour to Europe by coach or air had arrived and a steady decline in the number of foot passengers through the ferry ports set in. Today's scruffy and anonymous electric multiple unit boat trains feeding ferries now totally divorced from railway ownership are pathetic successors to the rakes of Southern coaches labelled 'Continental Express. Short Sea Route' which once pounded the main lines of Kent.

*Below:*
**In addition to the boat train service, Dover regularly handled VIP special trains carrying presidents and royalty to and from London. This classic scene, taken on 7 March 1950, shows the special conveying President Auriol of France to London approaching Shakespeare Cliff tunnel. The engine is blue-liveried 'Merchant Navy' No 35019** *French Line CGT* **brought from Nine Elms to the Eastern Section for the occasion.** *P. Ransome Wallis collection, National Railway Museum, York*

# Chapter 5

# The Kent coast expresses

In addition to the benefits it provided for the Continental Expresses, the SR investment programme of the 1920s created an improved infrastructure for the operation of the domestic services linking London with Thanet and the coast between Folkestone and Sandwich. These had until World War 1, always been regarded as poor relations of the boat trains. Equally significant was the rationalisation carried out at the same time in Thanet (Fig 5), which made it possible for a number of trains to and from London to work right round Kent with one crew on the 178-mile Charing Cross-Dover-Margate-Victoria circuit that earned for them the name of the 'rounders'. With these developments there emerged a timetable pattern that remained little altered until electrification.

A significant influence on the pattern of express services was the fact that well before 1939 the north Kent coast between Whitstable and Herne Bay had already become one of the major centres of long-distance commuting to London, despite being situated around 60 miles from the capital. Some commuting also took place from Thanet, especially from Margate and Broadstairs, but the extended journey time to these extremities of the system acted as a disincentive. South Kent had nothing comparable, relatively little daily travel to London taking place from beyond Tonbridge.

The early growth of commuting from north Kent can probably be explained in terms of a combination of factors, such as the availability of land suitable for residential development, the

*Below:*
**The main function of the Kent railway network today is to carry commuters, mainly to and from London. Many office workers now travel to Charing Cross and Victoria, but in steam days most of the traffic was handled by Cannon Street. In June 1958, before the removal of Sir John Hawkshaw's single arch roof, an evening rush hour scene features 'Schools' No 30920** *Rugby* **on the 5.05pm to Hastings, 'West Country' No 34021** *Dartmoor* **on the 5.14pm to Ramsgate and a diesel-electric unit waiting to form a later Hastings line train.** *R. C. Riley*

lack of much local employment apart from the holiday industry and the perception of individuals that this would be a pleasant place to live. The area probably appealed to several groups of potential commuters - for example those with high incomes seeking to live in a desirable place, those nearing retirement and looking to move to a smaller house or bungalow, and young families attracted by the prospect of living beside the sea and the lower price of houses compared with those in London and the suburbs. Their decisions would be influenced by transport factors, especially the comfort, frequency and cost of train travel. In this respect north Kent was a distinctly favoured area. As long ago as 1896 the LCDR provided businessmen with a 'City Express' at 5.10pm from Holborn Viaduct to Margate, Broadstairs and Ramsgate. A slip portion was detached at Faversham and served the intermediate stations to Ramsgate. An up service was also provided but tended to vary over the years in its days and times of operation. Later, the SECR introduced specially reduced first and second class season ticket rates between London and stations from Whitstable to Ramsgate, while in 1911 an Association of Regular Kent Coasters was formed. Compartments were reserved for them and the Association had 200 members by 1914.

These direct links with the City of London were developed both by the SECR and the SR, the trains running to Cannon Street via the St Mary Cray to Chislehurst loop, opened in 1904. By 1938 eight commuter trains from the Chatham line reached Cannon Street on Mondays to Fridays before 10.00am. They were the 5.47am and the 6.46am from Faversham due in at 7.39am and 8.41am respectively via the North Kent line, the 6.20am and the 6.29am from Ramsgate at 8.28am and 8.54am, the 7.46am from Faversham at 9.19am, the 7.25am and 7.35am from Ramsgate at 9.19am and 9.36am respectively and the 8.20am from Herne Bay at 9.56am. The Ramsgate and Herne Bay trains included Pullman cars and all except the 6.46am, 8.54am and 9.36am arrivals also ran on Saturdays, since most city offices still operated a five and a half day week. Seven down trains ran each evening from Monday to Friday at 4.32pm to Faver-

*Above:*
**In the 1930s the Thanet expresses were to a large extent in the hands of the 'King Arthurs', which remained in evidence after World War 2. No 776 *Sir Galagars* is seen leaving Margate on 7 June 1948. The lines on the left led to the goods depot.** *J. C. Flemons*

*Below:*
**The 'Lord Nelsons' based at Stewarts Lane in the 1930s mainly found employment on boat train traffic but were also sometimes used on the Ramsgate line. No 859 *Lord Hood* is seen approaching Herne Hill from the Brixton direction with a down express whose pre-grouping rolling stock suggests it is probably a summer extra.** *S. A. W. Harvey*

*Above:*

**Another scene from the 1930s finds 'J' class No 1599 leaving Ramsgate with the 10.06am from Margate to London via Canterbury West. This Pullman car train called at all stations to Ashford, where it joined a portion from Dover and was due in Charing Cross at 1.28pm. The hunky 'J' class once hauled suburban trains in the London area until, displaced by electrification, they found a home at Ashford. The last was withdrawn in 1951, by which time they were the final 0-6-4Ts to run in Britain.** *Revd A. W. V. Mace*

*Below:*

**A view of the 11.35am Victoria-Ramsgate, passing Bickley under Christmas card conditions behind No 34017 *Ilfracombe*. In winter the 11.35am had only two Pullman cars, the stock returning with the 5.05pm train from Ramsgate on a two hour schedule to Victoria.** *S. Creer*

sham, 4.45pm and 5.15pm to Ramsgate, 5.22pm to Dover and 5.47pm, 6.15pm and 6.23pm to Ramsgate. Three (the 4.32pm, 5.22pm and 6.23pm) were slow trains beyond Rochester, the others running non-stop to Faversham or Whitstable in around 70 minutes to the latter. On Saturdays, five trains from Cannon Street at 11.38am, 12.15pm, 12.46pm, 1.15pm and 1.20pm were provided for city workers returning to the coast.

These commuter trains represented about a third of the services on the Thanet line, the off peak trains running at hourly or sometimes two hourly intervals from Victoria, most conveying Pullman cars. The old main line between Faversham and Dover had by this time become the branch line, served mainly by stopping trains. However, it retained one off peak through service to Victoria, up at 9.22am from Dover Priory returning at 2.10pm to Dover Marine.

The Folkestone and Deal main line in the 1930s showed a much more even distribution of trains throughout the day. Only

three ran each morning from Monday to Saturday to Cannon Street, arriving at 9.24am from Ashford, 9.30am from Ramsgate and 10.11am from Margate. They were, of course, supplemented by Hastings line services between Tonbridge and London, while the 9.24am and 9.30am arrivals followed a time-honoured SECR practice by serving both Cannon Street and Charing Cross by way of the Southwark triangle. Four business trains left Cannon Street each evening from Monday to Friday at 4.38pm for Dover, 5.00pm for Ramsgate, 5.42pm for Ashford and 6.18pm for Ramsgate. Otherwise the service, after the departure of the early morning passenger and vans trains, consisted of expresses and semifasts from Charing Cross at 9.15am, 11.15am, 1.15pm, 3.00pm, 4.15pm, 5.15pm and 6.15pm (both Saturdays only), 7.15pm, 7.30pm (to Margate via Canterbury West) and 9.05pm. Up trains reached Charing Cross at 8.42am, 9.35am and 9.40am (via Cannon Street), 10.38am, 11.28am, 12.30pm, 1.28pm, 2.55pm, 3.46pm, 6.30pm, 8.23pm and 10.41pm. Of these, the 11.28am and 1.28pm came from Dover; the rest, like the down trains, were through services from Ramsgate and Margate via the coastal route. A journey time of around three hours to Thanet and the need to pay an additional fare for the 99 miles between London and Ramsgate via Folkestone compared with the 79 miles via Chatham meant that the trains on this route did not compete for

Thanet traffic with those on the LCDR route, which generally took around two and half hours. One train, the 3.15pm Mondays to Fridays Chatham line train from Victoria, had a 90 minute non-stop timing to Margate; this was extended to 96 minutes on Saturdays.

The fastest trains on the Ashford route were the 12.30pm and 6.30pm arrivals at Charing Cross and the 4.15pm and 7.15pm down. They were scheduled to run the 70 miles between Charing Cross and Folkestone Central in 80 minutes, with a stop at Waterloo East, and were known unofficially as the 'Folkestone Flyers'. Like most other trains on the route they conveyed Pullman refreshment cars.

It was on the Kent coast expresses that the 'Schools' class 4-4-0s introduced in 1930 did some of their best work in the prewar years. In 1936 12 (Nos 912-923) were allocated to Ramsgate and six (Nos 934-939) to Bricklayers Arms. They formed the front line motive power, duties they shared with the 26 'King Arthurs' allocated to Ramsgate, Dover and Stewarts Lane, although those at the latter sheds found extensive employment on boat trains. The large number of summer season extra trains also ensured a continuing role on expresses for the SECR 4-4-0s and the 'D1', 'E1' and 'L1' classes as well as a number of LSWR 'T9s' allocated to Stewarts Lane.

*Above left:*
**The postwar steam heyday is again recalled in this view of 'King Arthur' No 30768 *Sir Balin*, the 'Pride of Stewarts Lane', at Bickley junction on Saturday 19 March 1955, on its regular duty, the 3.35pm Victoria to Ramsgate express. It was the practice at Stewarts Lane at this time to roster regular engines to certain trains, a policy which paid off with good quality locomotive performance.** *S. C. Nash*

*Left:*
**An evening scene at Ashford on Tuesday 16 August 1955. Hither Green's immaculate 'King Arthur' No 30806 *Sir Galleron* has arrived with the 5.41pm business train from Cannon Street, as sister engine No 30804 *Sir Cador of Cornwall* approaches with the 4.55pm Margate to Charing Cross semi-fast.** *Mike Esau*

After World War 2, when Kent coast express services outside the early morning and rush hour periods were reduced to about six in each direction on each line, a service pattern much like that of the 1930s was resumed. Despite population growth in most of the towns of east Kent (by 22% at Herne Bay, 23% at Whitstable, 18% at Broadstairs and 10% at Ashford between 1931 and 1951) there were, by January 1959, only five morning commuter trains from Thanet to Cannon Street. They arrived at 8.23am, 8.54am, 9.19am, 9.36am and 9.56am, the first three running on Mondays to Saturdays and the others from Mondays to Fridays only. Seven still ran on Monday to Friday evenings at 4.31pm, 4.44pm, 5.14pm, 5.18pm, 5.44pm, 6.14pm and 6.24pm; on Saturdays only two trains ran to Thanet, at 12.45pm and 1.15pm, to cater for those who still worked a five and a half day week. On the Ashford line there were four business trains in each direction although an interesting development was that one of the up trains responded to the growth of office employment in the West End by running direct to Charing Cross, arriving at 9.40am. It consisted of one of the diesel-electric multiple-units that had taken over the Charing Cross to Hastings service from 1957. More of these units were used on the Folkestone line as steam was phased out in the years leading to electrification in 1961.

With Pacific motive power available there was pressure soon after the war to resume pre-1939 standards of speed on the expresses. As early as October 1946 the weekday 4.15pm and the 7.15pm from Charing Cross (along with the 12.55pm Saturdays only) were booked in 85 minutes to Folkestone, while in the up direction the 11.05am and 5.05pm from Folkestone had similar schedules. Restoration of the prewar 80 minute schedule came in June 1953, when the 9.40am from Margate, after serving all stations to Dover Priory, left Folkestone Central at 11.10am and reached Charing Cross, after a Waterloo stop, at 12.30pm. The title 'Man of Kent' was bestowed upon it and the 4.15pm down train, which also ran to Folkestone in 80 minutes and made a similar pattern of stops. This was the last regular Southern steam express to be given a name, the train having a life of only eight years. During this time a number of changes were made, notably from June 1956 when another pair of trains, the 12.40pm up from Margate and the 1.15pm down, also became the 'Man of Kent'. This resulted from the introduction of BR Mark 1 rolling stock, with the destination boards on the carriage sides immediately above the windows rather than on the roof as with Southern vehicles. At Charing Cross, where the train terminated in platform six against the station wall, it was difficult to remove the boards, leading to a decision to retain the name on the return working, the 1.15pm down! Neither the 12.40pm up nor the 1.15pm down were as fast to Folkestone as the original 'Man of Kent', since they made additional stops at Shorncliffe and Ashford. However, the 1.15pm was scheduled to reach Ashford in 60 minutes, probably the fastest ever steam hauled time.

Thereafter the train had a rather chequered history. In 1957, as a result of the new increased frequency Hastings line

*Left:*

**Despite the availability of many larger engines, the older Maunsell 4-4-0s still took a hand on express duties in the 1950s. One of the handsome 'L1' class, No 31754, based at Dover and regularly used to assist the 'Night Ferry', is seen at Sittingbourne with an up train in 1956.** *Mike Esau*

*Below left:*

**A regular 4-4-0 duty until the end of steam on the Folkestone line was the lightweight 7.24am London Bridge to Ramsgate passenger and van train, running fast between Tonbridge and Ashford before forming a slow train round the coast. 'D1' No 31739 is seen here during the Ashford stop. The train was frequently used to pass-out newly qualified locomotive crews, and one wonders whether the young man in the picture is receiving good news or bad from the locomotive inspector.** *Mike Esau*

*Below:*

**In a picture that evokes memories of one of the lost smells of the railway, that of steam heated coaches, Pacific No 34073 *249 Squadron* starts the climb up Hildenborough bank on a winter morning in 1959 with an up Folkestone line express.** *Mike Esau*

*Top:*
**A down express in the Vale of Kent in the last days of steam headed by 'West Country' No 34027 *Taw Valley*. Despite its Devon name the engine has a strong association with the Kent coast line. Allocated new to Ramsgate in 1946, she served there for two years before transfer to Exmouth Junction. After rebuilding in 1957, she returned to Ramsgate, later seeing service at Bricklayer's Arms and Brighton. Following scrapping, rescue and rebuilding, she returned again to Kent in 1991 and 1992 (Chapter 11).** *Mike Esau*

*Above:*
**In 1948 an all-Pullman train, the summer only 'Thanet Belle' returned to the Ramsgate line for the first time in over 20 years. It left Victoria at 11.30am on Mondays to Fridays, returning from Ramsgate at 5.5pm. It is seen here in charge of 'Battle of Britain' Pacific No S21C157 *Biggin Hill*.** *E. R. Wethersett*

diesel service the departure of the Folkestone line trains from Charing Cross was altered to 08 minutes past most odd hours. This affected the former 1.15pm departure while the 4.15pm 'Man of Kent' became the 4.10pm departure on an 82 minute timing to Folkestone. Some 80 minute Folkestone schedules reappeared late in 1959 but with work proceeding on the second stage of the Kent electrification, they were short lived.

Like many Folkestone line expresses the 'Man of Kent' was usually worked by light Pacifics from Ramsgate shed. The 'Schools' class, all of which were allocated to the SR South Eastern division by the mid-1950s, frequently deputised for them and were rostered for the 4.15pm down train, a Dover duty. As the steam fleet was run down in the early 1960s the train finished its life with diesel haulage, either a single or paired 'D5000' or 'D6500' types.

*Above:*
**When traffic was heavy, particularly on Saturdays, the 'Thanet Belle' Pullman train did not always qualify for Pacific haulage. It is seen here near Shortlands headed by 'King Arthur' No 30806 *Sir Galleron,* not even sporting a headboard.** *R. C. Riley*

On the Chatham line the restoration of prewar schedules to Margate was difficult, as population growth at intermediate stations required trains to make more stops. Best postwar times were therefore in the order of just over two hours from Ramsgate and 105 minutes from Margate to Victoria. The summer of 1948, however, saw the restoration of the first all Pullman service on this line since the depression killed off the Sundays

*Below:*
**The 1.08pm (formerly 1.15pm) down 'Man of Kent' passing London Bridge without the engine nameboard on Thursday 14 May 1959 headed by No 34021 *Dartmoor.* This train was named in 1956, the 4.15pm down having carried the title since 1953. The 1.08pm was not as fast to Folkestone as the latter train, since it called at Ashford and Shorncliffe.** *R. C. Riley*

only all first class 'Thanet Pullman Limited' 20 years earlier. The new train was the 'Thanet Belle', a summer only working booked to leave Victoria at 11.30am on Mondays to Fridays, reaching Margate at 1.17pm and Ramsgate at 1.34pm, returning from the latter at 5.05pm. Saturday timings were 3.05pm down and 8.20pm up. The train was usually of 10 Pullmans, two of them first class. From 1950 an additional Saturday working was added at the unreasonable hour for a Pullman of 7.55am in the down direction, returning as a lunch time train at 11.15am from Ramsgate.

In 1951, as part of the Festival of Britain celebrations, a change was made which affected the train for the remainder of its life. Somewhat optimistically, a Monday to Friday service to Canterbury East was provided by detaching three Pullmans at Canterbury. The name 'Thanet Belle' was not, therefore, strictly accurate and that of 'Kentish Belle' was substituted and retained when the service reverted to one to the Thanet resorts in the following year. The Canterbury service was not a commercial success and on the section south of Faversham received rather pedestrian treatment, being worked by any available engine and

carrying no headboard. A similar treatment was often handed out to the main train, especially on Saturdays when Pacifics were in short supply and engines ranging from 'Schools' and 'King Arthurs' to 'N' class moguls and 'Standard' class 4 4-6-0s worked the Pullman.

As a seasonal train serving holiday resorts the 'Kentish Belle' had more in common with the 'Devon Belle' than the year round 'Brighton Belle' and 'Bournemouth Belle' services and the 'Golden Arrow'. Like the 'Devon Belle' it was short lived, making its last run on Saturday 14 September 1958, leaving the 'Golden Arrow' almost alone to fly the Pullman flag on the Kent coast.

Thus the picture that emerges is one of a year round service between London and the Kent coast not significantly different after World War 2 from that provided before 1939. In contrast to the large number of trains provided in summer, especially on the Thanet line, Sunday services at other times of the year were poor. They catered mainly for day trips to the coast and for passengers returning to London on Sunday evenings, with gaps of three to four hours in the service at other times. Provision was at a particularly low level just after the war, with only seven trains each way on the Ramsgate line in October 1946. After the 12.35pm departure only two trains (at 3.35pm and 8.35pm) left Victoria for Ramsgate! Some improvement took place by the 1950s, with services restored to prewar levels but a general air of stagnation was setting in by this time.

The postwar years saw a continued improvement, however, in the quality of the rolling stock, non-corridor coaches usually only appearing in seasonal extra trains. The new coaches

*Left:*
**The 4.15pm down 'Man of Kent' was a regular duty for a Dover 'Schools'. No 30920 *Rugby* is seen near Tonbridge on Saturday 25 July 1953.**
*LCGB/Ken Nunn Collection*

*Below left:*
**In the last years of steam BR Standard engines made their appearance on the Kent coast lines, Class 5 4-6-0s Nos 73080-73089 being allocated to Stewarts Lane. No 73088, later named *Joyous Gard,* is seen departing from Faversham for Ramsgate on Sunday 4 May 1958. A local train for the Dover line is about to leave the platform behind a London Midland Region 2-6-4T.** *S. Creer*

*Above right:*
**The smaller BR Standard Class 4 Nos 75065-69, allocated to Dover, were less highly regarded than the Class 5s. However on the last day of steam the 5.02pm up train from Ramsgate, including Pullman cars and on a schedule of 129 minutes to Victoria (non stop from Whitstable), was entrusted to No 75065. The train is seen leaving Broadstairs.** *J. J. Smith*

*Right:*
**Not all the year-round express services from Kent went to London. The weekday through train to Birkenhead is seen on the Redhill to Reading line going great guns on the climb to Betchworth in March 1957 behind Class 4 No 76062. The nine coach load included coaches from Hastings and Brighton, attached to the Kent coast portion at Redhill.**
*Gerald Siviour*

**TABLE 1**

## S.R. BROMLEY SOUTH-CHATHAM

| Dist. | Engine No.<br>Load (Coaches)<br>Load (tons tare)<br>Load (tons gross) | Schedule | 30800 (a)<br>9<br>301<br>320 | | 73089 (b)<br>9<br>301<br>320 | | 73080 (b)<br>9<br>297<br>310 | | 34017 (c)<br>10<br>332<br>350 | |
|---|---|---|---|---|---|---|---|---|---|---|
| miles | | min. | m. s. | m.p.h. | m. s. | m.p.h. | m. s. | m.p.h. | m. s. | m.p.h. |
| 0.0 | BROMLEY SOUTH | 0 | 0 00 | — | 0 00 | — | 0 00 | — | 0 00 | — |
| 1.8 | Bickley Junc. ... | 5 | 5 20 | 30 | 4 42 | 33 | 4 27 | 44 | 9 59 | 31 |
| 3.9 | St. Mary Cray ... | — | 8 07 | 65/56/61 | 7 16 | 68/60/65 | 7 05 | 65/62/70 | 12 42 | 70/63/68 |
| 6.5 | SWANLEY ... ... | 11 | 10 46 | 56 | 9 45 | 60 | 9 30 | 16 | 15 06 | 64 |
| 9.6 | Farningham Road ... | — | 13 35 | 80½/64 | 12 21 | 85/74½ | 12 05 | 86/75 | 17 33 | 90/77 |
| 12.5 | Fawkham ... ... | — | 16 00 | 72/57 | 14 36 | 78½/63 | 14 10 | 78/65 | 19 39 | 81/66 |
| 15.1 | Meopham ... ... | — | 18 27 | 63 | 16 53 | 70 | 16 20 | 72 | 21 45 | 76 |
| 16.1 | Sole Street ... ... | 21 | 19 25 | 60 | 17 47 | 64 | 17 11<br>sigs. | 69/83<br>*40 | 22 35 | 71 |
| 20.1 | Cuxton Road ... | 26 | 22 43 | †80 | 20 58<br>sigs. | †84<br>*18 | 21 15 | — | 25 50<br>sigs. | †80<br>*24 |
| 22.2 | Rochester Bridge Jc. | 29 | 25 49<br>sigs. | *30/43<br>*8 | 24 42<br>sigs. | 40<br>*18 | 24 13<br>sigs. | *40/56 | 29 02<br>sigs. | 35<br>*25 |
| 23.4 | CHATHAM ... ... | 32 | 29 49 | — | 28 00 | — | 27 11 | — | 32 31 | — |
| 23.4 | Net times (min.) ... | 32 | 28½ | — | 26½ | — | 26 | — | ‡31¼ | — |

* **Speed restriction.**  † **Maximum down Sole Street bank.**  ‡ **26 min. with normal start.**
(a) " King Arthur " 4-6-0 *Sir Meleaus de Lile.*  (b) Class " 5MT " 4-6-0.  (c) " West Country " 4-6-2 *Ilfracombe*

designed by O. V. Bulleid and produced in large numbers shared most of the express duties with those designed by Richard Maunsell in the 1920s and 1930s. All were superb vehicles, the latter noted for their smooth riding and the comfort of the deep upholstery, while the Bulleid coaches, with their large windows made possible by not having doors in each compartment offered new possibilities for enjoying the passing scenery. Many were made up into three or four coach sets, as were the Standard Mk 1 coaches which appeared in the 1950s. The only real loss was in the catering provision, the Pullman cars which had in the prewar and early postwar years operated on many expresses, being replaced by less glamorous 'refreshment' and 'buffet' cars. However, as late as January 1959 an odd Pullman car working survived on the 11.35am Victoria-Ramsgate, returning on the up evening fast train at 5.02pm.

There can be no doubt that the 1950s represented the heyday of steam operation in terms of variety of engines to be seen. Although unrebuilt Wainwright 4-4-0s had virtually disappeared from regular expresses, the Maunsell rebuilds and the 'L1s' still had regular duties on both main lines, particularly on some early morning and passenger and van trains. Of the other Maunsell express engines, the 'Schools' in particular remained to the fore almost to the end of steam operation. The 'King Arthurs', on the other hand, were to some extent eclipsed by the arrival at Stewarts Lane during 1955 of a new batch of Standard Class 5 4-6-0s, Nos 73080-73089. They immediately appeared both on boat train duties and Kent Coast expresses, including the 3.35pm Victoria to Ramsgate, returning at 7.45pm. This had for several years been the regular duty of No 30768 *Sir Balin*, the 'Pride of Stewarts Lane', a gleaming 'King Arthur' whose condition matched that of the top boat train Pacifics. Another notable 'King Arthur' in the 1950s was that allocated to Hither Green for working the 5.41pm Cannon Street to Ashford, returning next morning with a goods train. As the only express engine allocated to this freight shed it was also kept cleaned to perfection. The engine was usually one of the 30800-30806 series, fitted with a six-wheeled tender.

The middle 1950s also saw the arrival at Dover of some of the smaller Standard class 4 4-6-0s, Nos 75065-9. They also appeared on express trains, one of them replacing a 'King Arthur'

**Table 1**
**Locomotive performance Bromley South to Chatham**
(Reproduced from *Trains Illustrated*, September 1956, p425)

on one of their last regular express duties, the 9.20am Dover Priory to Victoria, scheduled to run non-stop from Canterbury to Chatham. Nevertheless, the advent of the busy summer timetable inevitably brought the older engines back to express work.

An article by Cecil J. Allen (The Dover Road, *Trains Illustrated* 1950, pp76-82) provided a review of locomotive performance from pre-grouping days until the early postwar years. The picture that emerges is of a route which, with an overall speed limit of 85mph, severe gradients, sharp curves and the possibility of delays from suburban service in the London area made considerable demands on locomotives and crews if time was to be kept. Another article (*Trains Illustrated*, 1956 pp425) compares the performances of a 'King Arthur', Standard class 5 4-6-0s and a 'West Country' over the difficult 23 miles between Bromley South and Chatham (Table 1) showing all, especially the Standard engines, in a very favourable light.

Nevertheless, there was evidence by the mid-1950s of stagnation, journey times and service frequencies having shown little general improvement for many years. Comments also appeared in the railway press about poor timekeeping, even by the principal expresses such as the 12.40pm ex-Margate 'Man of Kent'. Things were destined to get worse as preparations were made for electrification and Ransome-Wallis (The Southern in trouble on the Kent coast, *Trains Illustrated*, April 1959, pp 212-220) provides a very gloomy picture of the last days of express steam on the Thanet line. Problems arose from a failure to modify timetables to take account of the inevitable delays associated with a major programme of track and signalling alterations (Chapter 11) and, with engines sometimes in poor condition, timekeeping suffered badly. This was a serious problem on a line heavily dependent on commuter traffic to provide a return on the capital invested in electrification, since late arrivals at the office could cost an individual his or her job. It was all rather a sad and chaotic end to the steam age and local people awaited with keen anticipation the start of the new electric services promised by the 1955 Modernisation Plan.

# Chapter 6

# Summer weekends

On spring and summer bank holidays today three or four additional electric trains are scheduled to run in the morning from London and its south eastern suburbs to Margate and Ramsgate, returning in the early evening. They provide a last reminder of what was in steam days, along with the provision for commuters, the lifeblood of the main line to Thanet — a huge traffic in holidaymakers and day excursionists who travelled this way to the resorts spread round the coast from Whitstable to Ramsgate. Although relief trains and excursions also ran on weekdays, especially during school holiday periods, it was at weekends that this traffic grew to a crescendo. It took several forms — an intense Saturday service taking holidaymakers to and from their annual week by the seaside, day and half-day excursion trips on Sundays and private trains for works outings, social clubs, Sunday schools and other organisations. Some of the excursions were hired by travel agents.

The attractions to the holidaymaker of the Kent coast were both natural and man made. While much consists of cliffs or muddy or shingle beaches, Thanet, in particular around Margate, Broadstairs and Ramsgate, is noted for the quality of its sands. Margate in particular benefited from the early establishment of a tourist industry, Thames steam barges bringing nearly 100,000 visitors in 1830. According to Simmons (*The Railway in Town and Country, 1830-1914*, p251) the coming of railways may initially have slowed down the town's development as it was served only by the circuitous route via Ashford and Londoners were given the chance of holidaymaking elsewhere. But when the LCDR direct route opened in 1863 Thanet was put back in the forefront of the London holiday trade and the rapid development of hotels, boarding houses and amusements followed. Not all the resorts were affected in the same way by the railways, Birchington, Westgate and Broadstairs remaining much quieter than Ramsgate and Margate.

Other parts of the Kent coast were also developed in different ways. Folkestone catered for family holidays but Deal and Sandwich, lacking sandy beaches, remained quieter and more

*Right:*
**In addition to the LSWR 'T9' 4-4-0s, the larger 'L12' class also worked for a while in Kent in the 1930s. No 417 is seen on a down train near Shortlands, the headcode indicating that it is bound for Ramsgate from Holborn Viaduct.**
*Revd A. W .V. Mace*

*Below right:*
**Just before World War 2, Brighton Atlantics, displaced by the mid-Sussex electrification, appeared on Kent coast trains. No 2426 *St Alban's Head* is seen leaving Bromley South on 30 July 1938 in the company of a birdcage 'long set'. The Atlantics did not stay long and after the war returned to their home pastures at Brighton and Newhaven to work boat trains and Oxted line business services.**
*H. C. Casserley*

urbane places where the golf courses and historic buildings were significant attractions. Later in the 1920s, holiday camps were developed at St Margaret's Bay north of Dover and on Romney Marsh and the Isle of Sheppey in response to a growing taste for organised entertainment. The SR also made its own rather ill-fated attempt in the early 1930s to develop a holiday resort at All-hallows, on the Isle of Grain. Served by a short branch from the Port Victoria line the estate developers went bankrupt and the lonely station on the Thames marshes failed to attract anyone but a few day trippers. It closed in 1961.

The climate also played a part in the development of the holiday industry on the Kent coast. Since Britain has its greatest summer warmth in the south and its greatest winter cold in the east, this south east corner experiences both extremes with a climate that verges on the continental type. It is therefore characterised by low annual rainfall (less than 25in) and a high percentage of sunshine hours (35-40% of daylight hours being classed as bright sunshine compared with a national average of 30%). Nevertheless, there are problems — notably that, like all east coast districts, the area is very exposed to cold winds from the east and the north, even in summer. Certainly the climate is not one that can compete with southern Europe, and Kent's holiday industry suffered badly when package tours opened up the Mediterranean resorts to a much greater cross-section of the British public in the 1950s.

In 1930 an estimated 30 million people took annual holidays in Britain and for many this meant a journey to the resort by train. In nearly all cases bookings were made from Saturday to Saturday, creating a weekly travel peak in addition to a seasonal one. Through the 1930s the number able to take holidays increased as a result of a rising level of real wages, although rail traffic to the Kent resorts came under considerable pressure from road competition due to the relatively short distance from London and the building of a new main road, the Thanet Way, in 1936.

Nevertheless, Table 2 shows just how intense was the service from London to the north Kent resorts on Saturdays in the late 1930s, 55 down trains leaving between 7am and 7pm and 58 arriving in London between 9am and 9pm — an average of a train approximately every 13 minutes in each direction. The service pattern was one of mainly down trains in the morning, arrivals in London being concentrated from mid-afternoon to mid-evening. This enabled most sets of coaches to make a round trip from London, where many were berthed in suburban sidings during the week, although some managed three Saturday journeys before being stabled at the coast until the next weekend. Although about half of the down trains had gone by noon, many people at this time still worked on Saturday mornings, a high service frequency therefore being maintained until around 3pm, after which arrivals came in thick and fast until after 8pm.

*Above:*
**Also displaced by electrification, Marsh 'I3' 4-4-2Ts put in an appearance in Thanet in the summer of 1938. No 2022 is seen heading an excursion train near Dumpton Park, Ramsgate.**
*Revd A. W. V. Mace*

*Left:*
**On summer Saturdays a number of trains started from Margate, allowing others to pass through non-stop to serve the smaller resorts. On the right of this picture 'U1' 2-6-0 No 1904 heads the 5.35pm to Victoria while 'Schools' No 922 *Marlborough* passes through with the 5.15pm from Ramsgate.**
*Revd A. W. V. Mace*

**TABLE 2**

**Saturday**

*Saturday Kent coast services via Chatham July 1938*

*Down trains 7am to 7pm*

*am*

| Time | Station | Destination |
|---|---|---|
| 7.38 | CX | to Ramsgate via North Kent Line |
| 7.55 | V | to Ramsgate (until 17 September) |
| 8.30 | V | to Ramsgate |
| 8.55 | V | to Ramsgate (first stop Whitstable) |
| 9.07 | Woolwich Arsenal | to Ramsgate |
| 9.10 | V | to Sheerness |
| 9.20 | V | to Ramsgate |
| 9.30 | V | to Ramsgate |
| 9.40 | Gravesend | to Ramsgate |
| 9.45 | Bromley South | to Ramsgate |
| 9.50 | V | to Margate (first stop Whitstable) |
| 9.58 | V | to Ramsgate |
| 10.06 | CS | to Ramsgate |
| 10.10 | V | to Margate |
| 10.15 | V | to Ramsgate (30 July to 3 September) |
| 10.25 | V | to Margate (until 10 September) |
| 10.35 | V | to Ramsgate PC |
| 10.45 | V | to Ramsgate PC |
| 10.45 | Herne Hill | to Ramsgate |
| 10.52 | CS | to Dover |
| 11.05 | V | to Ramsgate PC |
| 11.25 | V | to Ramsgate (until 10 September) |
| 11.30 | V | to Margate (30 July to 27 August) |
| 11.35 | V | to Ramsgate (16 July to 10 September) |
| 11.38 | CS | to Faversham |
| 11.40 | V | to Ramsgate |
| 11.50 | V | to Dover |

*pm*

| Time | Station | Destination |
|---|---|---|
| 12.05 | V | to Ramsgate |
| 12.15 | CS | to Ramsgate |
| 12.45 | CS | to Ramsgate |
| 12.45 | V | to Ramsgate (30 July to 10 September) |
| 12.46 | CS | to Sheerness |
| 12.55 | V | to Ramsgate PC |
| 1.15 | CS | to Ramsgate PC |
| 1.20 | V | to Ramsgate |
| 1.25 | V | to Ramsgate |
| 1.35 | V | to Sheerness |
| 2.04 | V | to Ramsgate |
| 2.15 | V | to Ramsgate PC |
| 2.25 | V | to Margate (until 3 September) |
| 2.35 | V | to Margate (until 17 September) |
| 2.50 | V | to Ramsgate |
| 3.05 | V | to Ramsgate (until 17 September) |
| 3.15 | V | to Ramsgate PC (non stop to Margate) |
| 3.20 | V | to Ramsgate PC |
| 3.30 | V | to Ramsgate |
| 4.15 | V | to Ramsgate |
| 4.34 | V | to Dover |
| 4.50 | LB | to Sheerness |
| 5.05 | V | to Ramsgate PC |
| 5.15 | V | to Ramsgate PC |
| 5.45 | V | to Sheerness |
| 6.05 | V | to Ramsgate (30 July to 27 August) |
| 6.15 | V | to Ramsgate PC |
| 6.55 | CX | to Faversham |

*Up trains 9am to 9pm*
*Arrival times in London*

*am*

| Time | Station | Origin |
|---|---|---|
| 9.02 | CX | from Ramsgate PC |
| 9.19 | CS | from Faversham |
| 9.19 | CS | from Ramsgate PC |
| 9.56 | CS | from Herne Bay PC |
| 10.25 | V | from Ramsgate PC |
| 11.27 | V | from Ramsgate and Dover |
| 11.34 | V | from Margate (until 17 September) |
| 11.45 | V | from Ramsgate PC |
| 11.55 | V | from Margate (30 July to 10 September) |

*pm*

| Time | Station | Origin |
|---|---|---|
| 12.01 | V | from Margate |
| 12.05 | V | from Ramsgate (23 July to 17 September) |
| 12.11 | V | from Ramsgate PC |
| 1.07 | V | from Dover |
| 1.19 | V | from Margate (until 17 September) |
| 1.26 | V | from Margate |
| 1.34 | V | from Ramsgate |
| 1.45 | V | from Herne Bay (30 July to 27 August) |
| 2.04 | V | from Margate (until 3 September) |
| 2.07 | V | from Ramsgate |
| 2.29 | V | from Dover |
| 2.42 | V | from Margate (until 17 September) |
| 2.48 | V | from Ramsgate |
| 3.29 | V | from Ramsgate (until 17 September) |
| 3.33 | V | from Ramsgate |
| 3.38 | HV | from Sheerness |
| 3.44 | V | from Margate |
| 3.48 | V | from Ramsgate PC |
| 4.00 | V | from Margate (23 July to 17 September) |
| 4.08 | V | from Ramsgate (until 17 September) |
| 4.14 | V | from Margate |
| 4.21 | V | from Ramsgate |
| 4.35 | V | from Herne Bay |
| 4.41 | V | from Margate PC |
| 4.55 | V | from Dover |
| 5.02 | V | from Margate |
| 5.13 | LB | from Margate |
| 5.24 | V | from Ramsgate |
| 5.28 | V | from Margate |
| 5.33 | V | from Herne Bay (until 17 September) PC |
| 5.44 | V | from Margate |
| 5.48 | V | from Ramsgate PC |
| 6.01 | V | from Margate |
| 6.23 | V | from Herne Bay (10 July to 10 September) |
| 6.34 | V | from Ramsgate |
| 6.49 | V | from Ramsgate (30 July to 27 August) |
| 6.52 | HV | from Margate (30 July to 3 September) |
| 6.55 | LB | from Ramsgate via north Kent line |
| 7.00 | V | from Ramsgate |
| 7.05 | V | from Ramsgate PC |
| 7.24 | V | from Margate PC |
| 7.28 | V | from Ramsgate |
| 7.30 | CX | from Sheerness |
| 7.42 | V | from Margate (30 July to 10 September) PC |
| 7.46 | V | from Ramsgate |
| 8.12 | V | from Dover |
| 8.23 | V | from Herne Bay (30 July to 3 September) |
| 8.27 | V | from Margate (16 July to 10 September) |
| 8.34 | V | from Ramsgate |

*Top:*
**The 'C' class 0-6-0s were great stalwarts of weekend passenger trains both before and after World War 2. No 1681 is seen with a matching set of SECR coaches on a holiday special near Dumpton Park in the 1930s.** *Revd A. W. V. Mace*

*Above:*
**In the 1930s multiple heading was a regular feature of summer weekends in Thanet in order to work the engines of trains which had terminated at Margate to Ramsgate shed for servicing. A 'King Arthur' on a train of non-corridor stock is seen being piloted to Ramsgate by 'Schools' class No 922 *Marlborough* and T9 class No 281.** *C. R. L. Coles*

In the down direction most trains went through to Ramsgate, only about six terminating at Margate and a few going to Sheerness, but in the up direction more than 20 started from Margate or Herne Bay. This enabled some of those starting from Ramsgate to miss out a Margate stop and serve the other smaller stations instead. Since most engines had to go to Ramsgate for servicing there was a great deal of light engine movement between Margate and Ramsgate, the locomotives often travelling in pairs to save paths or attached as pilots to other trains, producing triple-headed workings. In the London area some trains started from stations like Woolwich and Bromley South, others making roundabout journeys by suburban lines to call at places like Catford and Lewisham not normally served by main line trains. They then set out for the coast, often running non-stop to Whitstable. Similar roundabout journeys were made in the up direction

although the trains were usually booked to run through to the London terminals.

On the Folkestone line summer Saturday traffic to the resorts was nowhere near as dense as that to Thanet, although most of the boat trains went this way. The July 1938 timetable shows 21 down trains from Charing Cross between 9am and 5pm, with 14 arrivals between 11am and 8pm, the imbalance being explained by the fact that some down trains returned to London as 'rounders' via the LCDR route. Many of the Saturday extras were short workings to Deal or Folkestone, acting as reliefs to the normal through trains to Margate or Ramsgate, but an interesting up working was the 5.30pm arrival at Charing Cross of a through train from the New Romney branch. It consisted of nine coaches hauled by a 4-4-0, of which the 'L' class were the largest allowed on the branch. The service resumed after the war and was eventually taken over by a Hastings diesel electric set, but there was no corresponding down train either before the war or afterwards.

A comparison between the July 1938 timetable and that for July 1956 shows that, despite growing road competition, the number of trains between London and the north Kent resorts diminished only slightly in the postwar era; 51 down trains then left London between 7am and 7pm, with 49 up trains arriving

*Right:*
**In May 1959, towards the end of steam working, an immaculate 'N1' No 31876 takes the Catford loop through the attractive station at Denmark Hill with the 9.25am Victoria to Ramsgate express.** *R. C. Riley*

between 8am and 8pm. By this time, however, over a third of the trains were provided on a dated basis, running only at the peak of the season.

Most of the coaching stock used on the Saturday extras in the 1950s consisted of eight, nine or ten Maunsell vehicles displaced by Bulleid or Standard coaches from regular duties. Much interest centred, however, on the use of some surviving 'long sets' of mainly SECR non-corridor and semi-corridors which owed their longevity mainly to the summer weekend traffic. By 1955 16 'long sets' (given this label to distinguish them from the 3-coach 'Birdcage' sets still widely used on local trains at the time) remained; sets 334/5, 898, 901 and 918 had eight vehicles each, sets 519, 688, 696, 896/7, 900/6, 917 and 920 nine each and sets 636 and 346 had six and five coaches respectively. Only one had a regular duty — set 346, used on the Chislet colliery miners' train (Chapter 8). The rest were stored for most of the year at Maze Hill, Blackheath or Eardley Road carriage sidings and even on the busiest Saturdays sets 696 and 920 had no regular duties, being retained as spares for unadvertised extras.

Most of the other 'long sets' operated out and home workings from London, but four had three-leg diagrams which

*Above left:*
**The epitome of a summer Saturday at Victoria in the early days of British Railways. A down-at-heel 'E1' No 31506 heads a 'long-set' of shabby non-corridor coaches for the two-hour journey to the Kent coast. How many of its passengers, one wonders, resolved to go by coach next year?** *C. R. L. Coles*

*Above:*
**A busy scene at Bromley South in the summer of 1957. 'D1' No 31749, heading a down Ramsgate train consisting of an LSWR 'Ironclad' set, is passed by a Dover boat train headed by a 'Battle of Britain' Pacific.** *M. R. Galley*

left them at the coast or in London on alternate weeks, the former being stored at Martin Mill or Walmer. By this stage in their career the 40-50 year old coaches, many of which retained green paintwork applied in the 1930s, fell far below the standard of comfort that might encourage passengers to travel by rail rather than by road. Set 901, for example, had only seven compartments, five of them first class, with access to toilets, although perhaps there was compensation to be sought for some passengers

*Above:*

**Summer Saturday afternoons up to the late 1950s produced an endless stream of trains bringing holidaymakers back from the coast. Plodding up Sole Street bank in August 1958 is a 32 year old 'L1' class 4-4-0 No 31754, which has nearly made it to the top with nine corridor coaches of mixed vintage. The headcode indicates a train from the Dover line to Victoria.** *Gerald Siviour*

*Top right:*

**The weekend traffic kept many freight engines busy hauling empty stock between the terminals and suburban carriage sidings. On 7 July 1956 'C' class No 31692 heads out of Victoria over Grosvenor Bridge with the 3.50pm empty stock train to Blackheath consisting of LSWR coaches.** *J. J. Smith*

*Above right:*

**Some coaches had to return empty all the way to the coast, either to find berthing space or to form weekday commuter trains. The neat outline of Class 4 No 75067 shows to advantage in the low evening light as it approaches Factory Junction with a Victoria to Walmer stock train.** *R. C. Riley*

*Right:*

**Not all the trains heading up the Kent coast line on Saturdays were bound for London. On 27 July 1957 'Battle of Britain' Pacific No 34081 *92 Squadron* heads a train of Eastern Region Gresley stock, bound for the Midlands via the Great Central route, past Shortlands Junction. The Southern engine would work as far as Kensington via Factory Junction.** *R. C. Riley*

from the possibility of first class travel made possible by safety from the attention of travelling ticket inspectors! As the years went by several 'long sets' acquired Maunsell corridor stock, especially matchboard brakes once used on the boat trains, these replacing earlier birdcage brakes. Each year a few more 'long sets' were withdrawn, although some were still in use as late as 1958.

Although most holidaymakers travelling to Thanet came from the London area, one effect of the development of rail travel was to extend the hinterland from which visitors to the resorts came. By the 1930s a through train from the LMS, the 'Sunny South Special' from Manchester, and a through GWR train from Birkenhead to Thanet via Birmingham, Oxford, Reading and Redhill were established year round services, the latter running on weekdays and the former coming south on Saturdays, returning on Mondays. The LMS train ran in several portions at weekends and the GWR train in at least two portions. In the postwar years further services were added. By 1956, for example, trains were scheduled to reach Ramsgate at 6.28pm from Leicester and 6.56pm from Nottingham. travelling via the Great Central main line, Neasden and the West London line. On its return journey the Nottingham train ran through to Mansfield. Town holiday weeks in the north and the Midlands also produced extra trains; on 13 August 1955, for example, specials left Margate for Wolverhampton, Kidsgrove and Sheffield, some running via Canterbury, Maidstone East and Swanley to avoid congestion on the Chatham main line.

After the weekly Saturday migration the Kent coast line on Sundays and bank holidays was fully occupied with the movement of day excursions. Some trains originated at the main London terminals but many started their journeys at suburban stations before running fast to Whitstable and the other resorts, returning from Ramsgate in the middle or late evening. On some weekends use was made of Bricklayers Arms goods depot because it served a thickly populated area poorly served by passenger stations. Once again SECR 'long sets' played a major part in the excursions, some going through to the Thanet coast while others undertook shorter workings to Sheerness or Allhallows. The Sunday excursions also made extensive use of goods engines that otherwise would be idle, 'C' class 0-6-0s usually taking trippers to Allhallows from starting points such as Erith, New Cross and Deptford.

Not all of the excursions originated in south east London, however. Some were relatively short distance trips from towns such as Gravesend or Maidstone, while others came from resorts such as Brighton, with trains from Thanet going the other way. Some also originated in London's more distant suburbs. For example, between 1930 and 1937 a regular summer Sunday service ran between Kingston-on-Thames and Ramsgate, leaving about 8.45am and returning at 5.45pm from the coast. The train, of eight or nine coaches headed by a 4-4-0, was usually well patronised but ran for the last time on 5 September 1937.

Other excursions were of a more ambitious nature. In 1938 a works outing from Lancashire required five trains, leaving

*Above:*
**Extra inter-regional trains also ran via Redhill to the Western Region on summer Saturdays. 'Schools' No 30917 *Ardingly* is seen in a vintage harvest-time setting between Edenbridge and Godstone. The train of 12 ex-GWR corridor coaches would provide a considerable task for the engine on the next stage of its journey over the fierce gradients between Redhill and Guildford.** *Mike Esau*

*Below:*
**Sundays in the steam age produced a heavy flow of day excursions from suburban stations to the coast. In June 1954 'D1' No 31743 thunders through Beckenham Junction bound for Ramsgate with a train which had started its journey at Herne Hill.** *S. Creer*

*Bottom:*
**Sheerness, on the Isle of Sheppey, was a favourite destination for excursions, which were usually headed by 'Q' class 0-6-0s. On Whit Monday 1959, just before the start of electric working, No 30545 is seen at St Mary Cray with a trainload of day trippers.** *Ian Allan Library*

**Another Whit Monday 1959 excursion, this time from the Bexleyheath line via Gravesend, heads through the orchards near Teynham behind 'N' class No 31400. Your picture researcher is on the left of the photograph.** *Gerald Siviour*

on Friday evening and reaching Ashford around 8.00am on Saturday. The passengers then went forward to Margate by charabanc, the trains following empty to pick them up from about 4.00pm. The stock used included kitchen cars and several coaches of Lancashire and Yorkshire Railway origin.

Although the appearance of 'foreign' rolling stock in Kent was thus common before World War 2, SR engines were invariably used, although some were strangers to the area. For example, in 1938 ex-LBSCR I3s and 'Atlantics', displaced by the mid-Sussex line electrification, appeared. After nationalisation the use of engines from other regions became more common, Stanier Class 5 4-6-0s in particular being frequent visitors on Sunday excursions in the late 1950s.

All this rich pageant of railway activity came abruptly to a close in the summer of 1959 with the completion of the first phase of the Kent coast electrification. For a while unusual diesel engines and railcars came through with excursions but as travel habits changed and with a continued application of the Beeching philosophy of reducing assets these were doomed to eventual extinction. Sole Street bank on a summer Saturday or Sunday evening is now a very quiet place compared with the days all those years ago when an endless succession of elderly steam engines plodded their way to the summit with trainloads of homeward bound holidaymakers and day trippers.

*Above left:*

**Allhallows-on-Sea, on the Isle of Grain, was to have been a new resort and commuter settlement if Southern Railway plans of the 1920s had come to fruition. A short branch line was built to serve it and a station with long platforms provided for excursion trains. As the picture suggests, little development took place, and one wonders how a trainload of trippers deposited here on a wet Sunday were supposed to pass the time. Even the local service to Gravesend, here worked by 'H' class No 31193, ceased in December 1961 and a caravan park covers the site today.** *Mike Esau*

*Left:*

**In the 1950s Sunday excursions from north of London brought London Midland Class 5 4-6-0s to Kent on many weekends. A typical train is this one from Tring to Deal passing Bromley South behind No 45388.** *S. Creer*

*Above:*

**Not all excursions were bound for the seaside and Sunday specials to country stations for ramblers were popular. An example was this one from Victoria to the Hawkhurst branch on 28 May 1961. 'D1' No 31739 and 'E1' No 31067, the largest engines allowed on the line, are seen entering the delightful rural station at Goudhurst, the original terminus of the branch and now vanished without trace.** *R. C. Riley*

*Below:*

**A reminder of the roundabout routes taken by some excursion trains is provided by this New Cross to Ramsgate working headed by 'Schools' No 30924 *Haileybury*. The train is seen joining the Redhill to Tonbridge line by way of the now long vanished spur from the Oxted line. Its controlling signalboxes were especially opened on Sunday evenings in September for the passage of hop pickers friends' trains.** *Derek Cross*

# Chapter 7

# The Hoppers Specials

Even today fields of slender poles supporting a network of wires are a feature of the landscape in certain parts of Kent. They provide the infrastructure for the growing of hops, a crop introduced into England from Flanders in the 16th century when tastes changed away from the traditional English ale towards beer brewed with hops and having a more bitter taste. From then on the number of English hop gardens increased steadily and by the peak of the industry in 1878 they covered some 72,000 acres. Since that time the acreage has declined dramatically, the result of overseas competition and, in recent years, a further change away from beer towards lighter lagers, the brewing of which requires less hop input.

Although it is possible to grow hops over a wide area of Britain, Kent has always had the major concentration of output; other important growing areas were around Farnham in west Surrey and Ledbury in Herefordshire. The crop is tolerant of a wide range of soil and climate conditions but particular factors favoured its concentration in the south east. There was a ready supply of timber for poles and charcoal for drying while Kent

farmers, being among the most prosperous in England at the time of its introduction, could afford the high capital outlay for the establishment of hop gardens. Because of the importance of the Kentish woollen industry, Flemish weavers had settled here and could give advice to local growers from first-hand experience.

Although hop growing was well established before the coming of the railways, there is little doubt that improved transport gave added impetus to it, especially by making it possible to obtain the large amount of labour required for picking in late August and early September. Kentish baptismal records of the mid 17th century mention some 'strangers who came a hopping'

*Below:*
**The low-level platforms at London Bridge were the starting point for most of the specials provided for hop pickers and their families. Here 'L' class No 31769 awaits departure from platform nine on 6 September 1952. Being banned from some of the Kent branch lines because of their relatively high axle weight, the 'L' class were not often used on hop pickers' specials.** *J. J. Smith*

*Above:*

A vintage hoppers train of the early postwar years enters East Croydon station behind 'E' class No 1547 on 9 September 1950, bound for Kent via Oxted and the Crowhurst spur to the Redhill to Tonbridge line. Nearly three years after nationalisation, the engine still carried its Southern Railway number and lettering, and had probably been resurrected from storage among other ancient relics in the former LBSCR shed at New Cross Gate. *J. J. Smith*

*Right:*

In the early 1950s a Bricklayers Arms 'L1' 4-4-0 No 31787 is seen amid the hopfields on the main line at Tudeley, east of Tonbridge. The presence of several vans indicates that this a special to carry the hop pickers themselves rather than 'friends' who travelled to see them at weekends. *E. R. Wethersett*

*Below right:*

A Sunday afternoon in the postwar heyday of hop picking in 1951 finds 'D' class No 31734 and 'birdcage' sets Nos 576 and 596 waiting at Horsmonden on the Hawkhurst branch to form the 5.25pm hop pickers' friends' through special to London Bridge. The branch had no regular Sunday service and was specially opened for these trains. *J. J. Smith*

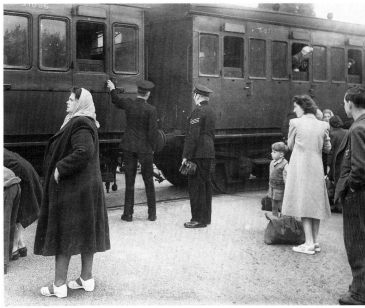

*Above:*

**The hop growing area of Kent extended into a part of Sussex served by the Kent and East Sussex Light Railway. This vintage scene features the arrival of the hop pickers at Bodiam station in the early 1950s. The local coal merchant's lorry has been cleaned up to take their belongings to the farms, while the pickers themselves walked with their improvised barrows. Although such scenes are long gone, Bodiam station survives in its original condition, a valued memorial of more leisurely days.** *Colonel Stephens Railway Museum, Tenterden*

*Above right:*

**As a major annual event in village life, the arrival of the hop pickers was attended by the local constabulary. The SECR non-corridors seen on the level crossing at Bodiam include No S971, now preserved on the Bluebell Railway.** *Colonel Stephens Railway Museum, Tenterden*

*Below:*

**Passing through the Darent valley near Eynsford on Saturday 22 September 1956, a classic hop pickers friends' special consists of six coaches of 'long' set No 917. The first coach is one of the rare 'birdcage' corridor vehicles once used on through services from the SECR to other railways.** *J. J. Smith*

(Filmer, R. *'Hops and hop picking'* p38), suggesting that even then there was insufficient local labour to harvest the crop. By the 19th century pickers were travelling regularly from London, the SER providing special trains for them, usually from Bricklayers Arms. In 1865 over 11,000 pickers were carried to and from the hop-fields and by 1880 the number had increased to around 20,000. By the 1920s, although the hop acreage had already substantially declined, the SR each year regularly carried around 35,000 people there and back on this annual migration. Hundreds of men, women, children, babies and dogs from the crowded docklands and industrial area of southeast London travelled for three weeks or so for a working, paid holiday in the fresh air of Kent. Local villagers tended to be wary of them, but the Londoners provided reliable labour and there were many records of families visiting the same hop gardens for generations. Living conditions were primitive, the pickers usually being housed in huts only rarely provided with such amenities as running water.

Equally primitive were the travelling conditions provided by the railways. The pickers had a reputation for violence and drunkenness so that only the oldest and most down-at-heel

**A reminder of the roundabout routes taken by the hoppers specials is provided by this photograph of 'U' class No 31639 approaching Selsdon with the 10.37am London Bridge to Maidstone West on 9 September 1950. The train had travelled from Lewisham over the line from Woodside to Selsdon which was closed in 1983, although the siding on the right remains to serve an oil terminal.** *J. J. Smith*

rolling stock was made available to them. The first train in 1856 is said to have consisted of cattle trucks and in the mid 1930s they were formed mainly of ex-LCDR six-wheelers dragged out of the reserve stock sidings at Crystal Palace High Level, Maze Hill and Blackheath. After the war and well into the 1950s ex-SECR 'long sets' were used, while vans for the vast quantities of luggage the pickers took with them were an essential feature of the trains. Sometimes two-coach push and pull sets from the country branch lines were taken up to London for the specials, while in 1955 and 1956 the Southern was so short of stock that rakes of ER carriages had to be borrowed. Only at the end of the 1950s were the hoppers treated to the luxury of Maunsell corridor stock, providing a degree of comfort undreamt of by earlier generations.

The main area concentrating on hop growing was in mid Kent, stretching northwards from Paddock Wood along the Medway Valley towards Maidstone and southwards along the Hawkhurst branch. A second major concentration was in east Kent around Canterbury and Faversham, but, perhaps because it is on a main line relatively well provided with service trains, this district did not attract the same number of hoppers specials as the Paddock Wood area. It was also well served by road and many hoppers arrived in London buses hired for the purpose.

As the end of August approached, the farmers decided the date on which they would begin picking. This was then notified to a joint committee of railway representatives and farmers set up to co-ordinate transport arrangements. A programme of special trains was organised and a postcard sent to the hoppers telling them the date and time of their trains. They would then make their way, with most of their worldly possessions loaded on to prams and wheelbarrows, to the originating stations, usually London Bridge or New Cross. The trains usually departed in the early morning, providing colourful and animated scenes in stark contrast to those shortly afterwards when the city-bound gentry with their briefcases and rolled umbrellas passed through. On arrival at the country stations there were more lively scenes as luggage was unloaded and piled on to farm wagons for the last stage of the journey and frantic searches were made for lost children. After about three weeks there were similar scenes when the pickers returned to London, usually by special afternoon or evening trains.

Carrying the pickers themselves was not the only function the railways performed because, in those days before paid holidays became general,most of the menfolk stayed behind in London, travelling to visit their families at weekends. A programme of 'hop pickers friends' excursions was therefore laid on, with down trains leaving London early on Saturday afternoons

and Sunday mornings, a stream of up trains making their way back on Sunday evenings. For example, on September 16 1951 no fewer than 21 'friends' specials' reached London between 6.37pm and 10.01pm, platforms 8, 9 and 10 being especially set aside to deal with them, while many of the regular expresses and boat trains were sent via Maidstone East to clear the main line for the hoppers.

The 'bottom of the barrel' rolling stock was matched by the engines used, for in those days the busy summer timetable lasted well into September and the locomotive stock was much depleted by the demands of boat trains and seaside holiday traffic. The hoppers' trains were therefore powered by anything that was left over, the engines coming from Bricklayers Arms (which drew on the collection of ancient relics normally stored in the old Brighton shed at New Cross Gate), Hither Green, Tonbridge and Ashford. During the 1946 season 114 special trains were run for the hoppers and their friends, the engines used being:

'B1' class 4-4-0s: 1217, 1445/6, 1450/3/4/5.
'F1' class 4-4-0s: 1028, 1031, 1062, 1156, 1205.
'D' class 4-4-0s: 1477, 1488, 1490, 1549, 1574, 1726/8, 1732/4/8.
'D1' class 4-4-0s: 1545, 1735/6.
'E' class 4-4-0s: 1036, 1159, 1166, 1175/6, 1515/6, 1547.
'E1' class 4-4-0: 1504.
'L' class 4-4-0s: 1776/8.
'L1' class 4-4-0: 1785.
'N1' class 2-6-0s: 1879, 1880.
'U' class 2-6-0: 1625.
'C' class 0-6-0s: 1225, 1580, 1714.

The appearance of so many 4-4-0s and 0-6-0s is partly explained by the fact that these were the largest engines allowed on the Hawkhurst branch, from which up to six through trains ran on busy days. This was due mainly to the very short shunting neck at the terminus and ensured that these small engines had a hand in operating the hop-pickers' trains right up until their last years. They also worked to the end on the Maidstone West line, although as the 1950s progressed more Maunsell Moguls and

*Above:*
**Paddock Wood, traditional centre for hoppers traffic, on 30 August 1958. By this time hand picking in the remaining hopfields was declining rapidly and with it the volume of pickers traffic. Also reduced to a few survivors were the SECR 'long sets' of which No 636 is seen behind 'D1' No 31735, forming a special to the stations along the Maidstone West branch.** *Gerald Siviour*

'Schools' 4-4-0s were used on trains bound for main line destinations like Pluckley and Headcorn.

Perhaps the greatest concession to hoppers' trains came in 1952 when a really modern engine, a Standard 2-6-4T from Tunbridge Wells West, took 'long set' No.903 empty to Paddock Wood early on Sunday mornings. It then made trips to Maidstone West and Headcorn before working the 5.10pm Staplehurst to London Bridge via Oxted, returning with the empty stock via Orpington.

Another oddity of the hoppers trains was the great variety of routes they took to reach London from Paddock Wood. Some ran direct up the main line via Orpington, but a few went via Swanley. Others set out in the opposite direction and reached London via Maidstone West, Strood and the Dartford loop. However, a favourite route which kept these wayward trains out of the way of more illustrious contemporaries was via the Redhill line from Tonbridge or, in most cases, round the little-used Crowhurst spur to join the Oxted line north of Lingfield. This spur, long since lifted, was double track and its controlling signalboxes were especially opened on Sunday evenings for the 'hoppers friends' trains. From Oxted, two routes to London were available; most trains ran via East Croydon, but a few went from Selsdon over the now closed route through Woodside to reach London Bridge via Lewisham.

The menfolk who packed into the specials were renowned for their heavy consumption of the liquid their families were helping to produce and on these roundabout journeys in non-corridor stock, nature's needs posed problems. They did not stand on ceremony. The stop at Oxted for engine watering was the cue for compartment doors to be flung open and nature's call answered from the doorways!

In the early postwar years there was a short lived slight increase in the acreage planted with hops, while the yield per acre continued to increase. Hoppers traffic therefore remained at a high level, but as the 1950s wore on rising living standards meant that fewer people went hopping and those who did found road transport more convenient to carry them and their belongings. The farmers, faced with increasing problems of finding labour, introduced machine picking and by 1957 over half the crop was gathered in this way. The days of hoppers' trains were clearly numbered. Where 10 years earlier 20 or more packed trains had made their way back to London Bridge on Sunday evenings, only about six ran on Sundays in the 1958 season and these were poorly patronised.

The Hawkhurst branch saw its last through 'hoppers' specials' in 1959 and the final trains ran in 1960. Traffic had reached a low ebb, with just a handful of trains serving the Maidstone West branch and the main line stations in the Vale of Kent. As the last hop pickers made their way home to London that autumn the curtain finally came down after over a century on one of Kent's most colourful and distinctive railway traffics.

*Below left:*
**In the last days of hoppers traffic not all trains ran through to London Bridge. In a siding at Paddock Wood, 'C' class No 31590 waits with a motley collection of rolling stock to provide a connection off a train from London Bridge. The regular Hawkhurst branch train consists of 'H' No 31184 with two ex-LSWR low roof corridors.** *Gerald Siviour*

*Below:*
**On Sunday 13 September 1959 the final hop pickers friends' special train ran from the Hawkhurst branch, closed two years later, to London Bridge. The train is seen leaving Cranbrook behind a neglected 'C' class No 31293, from Bricklayers Arms shed.** *Mike Esau*

# Chapter 8

# Stopping trains

Making generalisations about stopping train services in steam age Kent is difficult, for over the years there evolved a very irregular and complex pattern, with many through services across the network. Examples of such a journey were a 6.05am Reading to Margate (reached at 11.39am) via Redhill, Tonbridge and Dover, through trains between Ramsgate and Hastings via Canterbury West and Ashford and between Sevenoaks and Brighton via Tunbridge Wells West. Another roundabout but fascinating journey was provided by the weekday 2.42pm Margate to Cannon Street, a regular 'Schools' class duty in the 1950s: it called at all stations (except Margate East and Warren Halt) round the coast to Ashford before running via Tonbridge and Redhill to reach Cannon Street at 6.52pm. The year round weekday through train between Birkenhead (dep 7.40am) and Ramsgate also assumed the role of a stopping train after reaching Kent via Reading, Redhill (where a portion for Brighton and Hastings was detached) and Tonbridge. At Ashford it divided, one part going via Canterbury West to Margate and the other, usually of only two coaches, to Folkestone before calling at most stations to Ramsgate (reached at 5.10pm).

The spread of suburban electrification from London reached Maidstone East and the Medway towns in July 1939. Thereafter these places generally became the interchange points where stopping trains from the country end of the line usually ter-

*Left:*
**A vintage country junction scene from SR days features 'H' class No 1320 arriving at Minster with an Ashford to Margate train via Canterbury West. The small town of Minster grew around its abbey. Trains from the Deal line once reversed here to reach Ramsgate, but following the reopening of the east curve of the triangle in the 1920s, Minster's role as a junction was gradually reduced so that it is now little more than a wayside station.** *Revd A. W. V. Mace*

**TABLE 3**

*Stopping train services Tonbridge to Ashford 1938 and 1959*

**Monday to Friday from Tonbridge**
**July 1938**

*am*
6.30 to Margate via Canterbury West
7.40 to Dover (6.24 from Cannon Street)
8.45 to Margate
10.10 to Margate via Canterbury West

*pm*
1.07 to Ashford (12.05 from Charing Cross)
4.10 to Ashford
5.27 to Dover (4.38 from Cannon Street)
6.37 to Ashford (5.42 from Cannon Street)
7.10 to Margate (off 6.18 from Cannon Street)
8.28 to Margate (7.30 from Charing Cross)
10.18 (from Paddock Wood) to Ashford

**January 1959**

*am*
6.33 to Dover (4.50 from London Bridge)
7.34 to Dover (6.20 from Cannon Street)
8.49 to Margate (6.05 from Reading)
10.14 to Ashford

*pm*
12.59 to Ashford (11.46am from Charing Cross)
4.12 to Margate
5.28 to Folkestone (4.36 from Cannon Street)
6.33 to Ashford (off 5.47 from Cannon Street)
7.13 to Ashford (off 6.21 from Cannon Street)
8.32 to Ramsgate (7.30 from Charing Cross)
10.12 to Ashford

**Monday to Friday from Ashford**
**July 1938**

*am*
6.43 to Charing Cross
7.27 to Cannon Street and Charing Cross
8.30 to Cannon Street (from Margate)
9.30 to Tonbridge
10.42 to Tonbridge

*pm*
12.45 to Tonbridge
4.25 to Charing Cross
6.13 to Tonbridge
9.08 to Tonbridge

**January 1959**

*am*
6.41 to Tonbridge
7.33 to Charing Cross
8.03 to Cannon Street (from Rye)
9.30 to Tonbridge
10.40 to Tonbridge

*pm*
12.42 to Tonbridge
4.25 to Tonbridge
6.00 to Tonbridge (from Dover)
9.42 to Tonbridge

minated, passengers continuing their journeys to London by steam expresses or, in the case of the Maidstone East line, by stopping electric trains. On the SER route many locals started from or terminated at Tonbridge, although for over 25 years, between 1935 and 1961, Sevenoaks was the end of the electrified line. But the distinction was never a rigid one and Table 3 shows that a number of stopping trains, particularly in the early morning and rush hours, continued to and from London. Some expresses, for example the 5.47pm and 6.21pm from Cannon Street in the 1959 timetable, detached three coaches at Tonbridge to go forward calling at all stations to Ashford, enabling the main train to make a faster journey to the coast.

Local services in east Kent were much affected by the rationalisation of the routes in Thanet in the 1920s. Stopping trains over the former Dover and Deal Joint Line were henceforward provided mainly by trains from London to Folkestone which continued round the coast (calling at most stations) to Margate and Ramsgate, usually via the Minster avoiding loop, which re-opened in 1927. On the former LCDR main line the pattern of service evolved to one where most London trains contin-

ued round the coast to Margate and Ramsgate, the original main line to Dover becoming the branch line, generally served by local trains originating or terminating at Faversham or in the Medway towns.

A comparison of the stopping train service between Tonbridge and Ashford over a 20 year period illustrates some general characteristics of Kent local train services. It is apparent how irregular the services were, with gaps of around three hours between trains in the middle of the day and in the evenings. One or two extras ran on Saturdays but Sunday services were very scanty, with only two or three stopping trains in each direction. The same characteristic was repeated on other lines. On the ex-LCDR main line east of the Medway Towns there were gaps in the stopping service between Chatham, Sittingbourne and Faversham of three or four hours. It meant that, at this time when people depended much more on public transport than they do today, many wayside stations had very poor services indeed. For example, Rainham, today a sprawling commuter settlement, had only two down weekday trains (at 11.00am and 1.07pm) between the 8.38am to Ramsgate and the 4.48pm to Sittingbourne. Teynham fared even worse, with only two down trains between 9.00am and 6.04pm. It all emphasises the dramatic change brought about by electrification, when at least an hourly train on all lines became the norm and puts into perspective complaints about today's level of public transport provision. The Maidstone East to Ashford line was something of an exception. With around 14 trains a day in each direction in the 1950s there were few gaps of more than two hours between trains, although no expresses ran this way.

Table 3 also shows how unchanging was the pattern of services, the stopping trains running at almost identical times over the 20 year period. Even during the war there was little change and the conclusion seems to be that either the service provided was very well adjusted to local needs or else railway management was unresponsive to the challenge of changing times,

*Below left:*
**Local services right up to the 1950s frequently employed three coach sets of SECR coaches with their distinctive 'birdcage' lookouts in the brake vehicles. A lovely vintage train of two such sets, hauled by 'F1' class 4-4-0 No 1188, a Stirling engine rebuilt by Wainwright, is seen leaving Bromley South for Maidstone East in 1932.**
*L&GRP No 11270/Courtesy David & Charles*

*Below:*
**Another 'birdcage' set forms this Margate to Hastings local passing Margate East on Monday 25 May 1953 behind 'H' class No 31326. This station was one of only a small number on the main lines of Kent to be closed, this taking place soon after the photograph was taken.**
*S. C. Nash*

**Standard Mark 1 coaches also appeared in the 1950s on stopping trains such as this Dover to Faversham local leaving Shepherdswell in April 1959 behind 'L' class 4-4-0 No 31780.** *Gerald Siviour*

particularly with the growth of private motor transport in the 1950s.

Among purely local services were the miners trains which operated on two routes in east Kent; some were available for use by members of the public with a sense of adventure. The full development of the coalfield in the years after World War 1 brought many migrants to the area from other mining areas such as Somerset, North and South Wales, the Forest of Dean and Yorkshire where employment was declining. Some went to live in existing villages or in new purpose built settlements like Aylesham (Chapter 2), but others preferred, despite some hostility towards them by local people, to set up home in the larger towns such as Ramsgate, Deal and Dover.

The collieries generally worked three shifts — 6.00am to 1.45pm, 2.00pm to 9.45pm and 10.00pm to 5.45am — requiring the provision of special trains to get the men to work at what

**Not often seen on local trains in Kent were the ex LBSCR 'E4' class 0-6-2Ts, although they were sometimes employed on shunting duties. No 32507 from Redhill shed is seen leaving Edenbridge on 8 October 1951 with a local for Tonbridge along the original SER main line. All the wayside stations along this route have now been reduced to platforms with 'bus stop' type shelters.** *S. C. Nash*

**In the early 1950s, London Midland Region 2-6-4Ts, forerunners of the BR Standard 2-6-4Ts, were built at Brighton and put to work on local services. No 42097 is seen on Sunday 13 March 1955 with a Margate to Ashford local at Wye, still to this day an attractive wayside station with semaphore signals and a manually operated signalbox.** *John Head*

**Teynham, in the heart of the orchard country west of Faversham, was one of the many wayside stations in Kent to have a very indifferent service in steam days. The 12.35pm Victoria to Ramsgate train was one that stopped here and 'Schools' No 30910 *Merchant Taylors* is seen coming to a halt in April 1959. Although the platforms had been extended for an enhanced service of electric trains, gas lighting still survived.** *Gerald Siviour*

**Among the last new steam engines to be introduced into Kent were the British Railways Standard Class 2-6-2Ts, which entered service at Ashford shed in 1957. No 84026 is seen in 1960 in Folkestone Warren with a stopping train from Maidstone East.** *Mike Esau*

**A more unusual sight on a local train was this 'Q1' class 0-6-0 No 33012, seen near Staplehurst with a Tonbridge to Ashford train in 1960. Allocated to Feltham, the locomotive was probably running in after overhaul at Ashford works.** *Mike Esau*

would today be regarded as unsocial hours. The May 1948 working timetable shows the following miners' trains:

5.12am, 1.12pm and 9.20pm Margate and Ramsgate to Canterbury West for workers at Chislet Colliery.

6.57am, 3.04pm and 11.05pm Canterbury West to Ramsgate and Margate.

5.34am from Dover Priory and 3.00pm from Shepherdswell to Canterbury East for workers at Snowdown Colliery.

6.20am from Canterbury East to Dover and 1.30pm Canterbury East to Shepherdswell.

The early morning trains ran on Saturdays as well as Mondays to Fridays, while on Sunday evenings trains ran at 10.35pm from Margate and 9.06pm from Dover to cater for those going on the night shift.

Being short out-and-home workings, tank engines, particularly 'H' class and latterly LMR 2-6-4Ts were usually employed on the miners trains to avoid tender first running, although this was sometimes necessitated by the use of light Pacifics from Ramsgate shed on the Margate to Canterbury trains. Not surprisingly, the oldest available rolling stock was used, including ex-LCDR six-wheelers, while in the 1950s the Chislet Colliery train regularly employed ex-SECR non-corridor

*Above:*

**A memory of the Margate to Canterbury West services which for nearly 40 years ran three times daily from Monday to Friday for the miners at Chislet colliery. Consisting of ex-LCDR six wheeled coaches, the train is seen leaving Ramsgate in the 1930s behind 'H' class No 1016. What was then the new engine shed, with its coaling plant and water tower, is seen in the right background.** *Revd A. W. V. Mace*

'long set' No 346. A journey in one of the grubby and faded compartments of this train in the early hours of a dark, wet winter morning among men facing the prospect of eight hours down the pit and not seeing daylight for a week must have been an excruciating experience.

Most of the miners trains lasted until the end of the steam age but there was no place for them when new electric trains were introduced. In any case private transport and buses took over their function until the coalfield was itself killed off some 30 years later (Chapter 9).

*Below:*

**A 1950s view of the miners train, consisting of the then usual 'long set' and a 2-6-4T, entering Chislet Colliery Halt. The photograph emphasises the rural setting of the Kent coalfield and the high average age of the miners, many of whom came to the area in the 1920s from other declining coalfields. Chislet Colliery closed in 1969 and the whole east Kent coalfield is now just a memory.** *Revd A. W. V. Mace*

# Chapter 9

# Freight traffic

Apart from a small and now defunct coalfield, Kent lacks the significant mineral deposits which, in other parts of the country, gave rise in the steam age to major flows of trainload freight. The traffic pattern was, therefore, one of the movement of assorted mixed loads of up to 65 wagons between London terminals such as Bricklayers Arms and Blackfriars and sorting sidings such as Herne Hill and Hither Green, through marshalling yards in Kent to goods yards in the main towns or to sidings serving the region's industries. From the main marshalling yards at Tonbridge, Ashford and Hoo Junction, or smaller ones such as Keylands Yard at Paddock Wood, pick-up goods trains served the wayside stations and branch lines.

The county's diverse agriculture gave rise to important freight traffic in the past. Van specials conveying fruit and vegetables operated on a seasonal basis from east Kent to south London while Ashford, with one of Britain's largest livestock markets, dealt with over 70,000 animals a year in the west yard. In summer up to five livestock specials a day were handled, while each autumn around 30,000 sheep from Romney Marsh were sent to drier grazing areas elsewhere for the winter, returning in spring.

After World War 2 agricultural produce also made up a large part of the traffic arriving at Dover by train ferry from Dunkirk. Ten paths a day were available to take ferry wagons to various terminals, particularly Southwark and Battersea, in south London. These trains were among the few fully fitted freights operating in Kent. They consisted of up to 19 wagons, often with a 27ton brake van, giving loads of just over 400 tons. 'King Arthurs' and 'Schools' class were the usual motive power, although in September 1952 a 'WD' class 2-10-0 from Scotland, No 90757, was used as part of some test running on the SR.

*Below:*

**The major goods depot in south east London was at Bricklayers Arms, served by a busy branch from both the LBSCR and SER main lines into London Bridge. At North Kent West Junction on the branch 'W' class No 31919 heads a transfer freight for Norwood yard past the imposing signal cabin on Saturday 29 March 1958.** *R. C. Riley*

*Left:*
**Near the terminus of the Bricklayers Arms branch was a large motive power depot with an allocation of around 100 engines. Most were goods and mixed traffic types, along with passenger tank engines, but a number of the 'Schools' class were also based there for working the Hastings and Kent coast expresses out of London Bridge, Charing Cross and Cannon Street. On 28 February 1957, No 30929 *Malvern* basks in the winter sunshine outside one of the several sheds that made up the depot.** *R. C. Riley*

In the steam age the main concentration of manufacturing industry in Kent stretched along the south bank of the Thames from Dartford and Gravesend to Rochester and Chatham and then up the Medway Valley through Snodland and Aylesford towards Maidstone. Cement and paper making were the dominant activities, both long-established and pre-dating the railways. They were mainly carried on in relatively small scale works, the majority served by their own railway sidings. Both were heavy consumers of fuel and therefore had a considerable intake of coal; the products were distributed by rail all over southern England and, in the case of cement, as far beyond as Scotland. Further east, Sittingbourne, Faversham and Sheerness were industrial towns which handled considerable quantities of freight traffic, producing the flow of goods trains on the local railways shown in Fig 8.

The industrial area was served by the large marshalling yard at Hoo Junction, on the bleak and windswept north Kent marshes east of Gravesend. The down yard consisted of three dead-end and three through sidings in the angle between the Isle of Grain branch and the main line, but in 1928 a bigger one was added on the up side, consisting of up and down reception sidings, six marshalling roads and two others, one with a weighbridge and another for crippled wagons. The increasing traffic of wartime brought the addition of further sidings, so that at its peak there were 14 dead-end sidings as well as reception roads. In the early 1950s the yard handled around 2,000 wagons a day, requiring three shunting engines, usually two 'C' class 0-6-0s and a 'Z' class 0-8-0T. Although much reduced in size Hoo Junction remains open today, one of only two revenue earning marshalling yards surviving in Kent, the other being at Dover Town.

Over 40 trains left the yard during each 24-hour period in the early 1950s. Many served local yards and factories but there was also an important through traffic via the Medway valley line to Tonbridge. Many then ran to Redhill (to make connection with the central section of the SR) and over the Guildford line and on to Woking or Reading. Some originated at Anger-

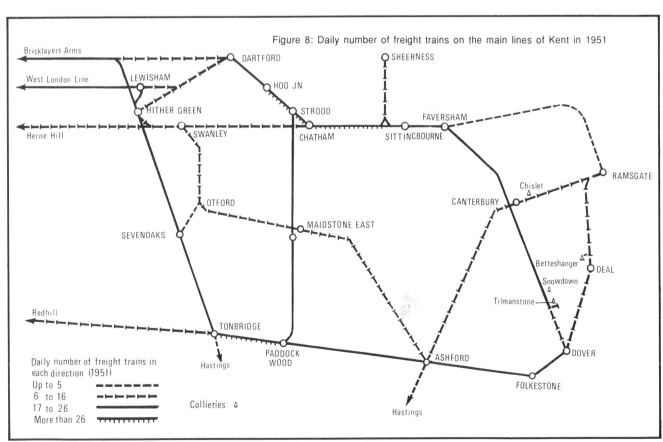

Figure 8: Daily number of freight trains on the main lines of Kent in 1951

Daily number of freight trains in each direction (1951)
Up to 5
6 to 16
17 to 26
More than 26

Collieries ᐃ

In the 1930s the Southern Railway developed a scheme for keeping as much daytime freight as possible out of the way of electric trains in the London area by using a cross country route from Guildford to Paddock Wood and Hoo marshalling yard. Near the western end of the route 'N' class No 31870 battles uphill towards Reigate in 1960 with a heavy mixed freight bound for Redhill. Note the use of lamps to provide the headcode rather than the usual SR discs. *Mike Esau*

The middle section of the Guildford to Hoo route made use of the old main line between Redhill and Tonbridge. 'Q1' No 33029 is seen at speed with a westbound freight near Penshurst in 1959. *Mike Esau*

From Paddock Wood the Guildford to Hoo route was via Maidstone West and Strood. On the picturesque line through the hop gardens and orchards of the Medway valley near Wateringbury 'N' class No 31860 heads northwards in August 1958. *Gerald Siviour*

Local goods trains sometimes provided employment for engines near the end of their career and displaced from more illustrious duties. 'E' class 4-4-0 No 31516, seen here approaching Ashford West goods yard from Maidstone in 1951, had sadly fallen from grace from the days when the class provided power for the top rank Continental expresses. *Derek Cross*

stein Wharf, on the south bank of the Thames near Charlton, the whole route playing a major part in a scheme devised as suburban electrification spread to keep as much daytime freight as possible away from the heavily used lines of the London area. Hoo yard was particularly busy at night and a special halt was provided so that crews could reach this remote spot by service and staff trains at all hours of the day and night.

Of the south east London goods depots, Bricklayers Arms was much the busiest. For today's commuter travelling along the Greenwich Railway arches on the way out of London Bridge (Chapter 2) the rusted rails of the Bricklayers Arms branch dropping to the south on a brick arcade from the vicinity of North Kent East Junction give no clue to the former importance of the branch. Although regular passenger services were short lived, it gave access to extensive carriage sidings at Rother-hithe Road, an engine shed with an allocation of around a hundred, various sorting sidings and Bricklayers Arms goods depot. This was amalgamated in 1932 with the nearby former LBSCR Willow Walk depot, the combined terminals receiving 550 wagons a day and forwarding 700. The arches near the Greenwich viaduct may one day carry passenger trains as part of an expanded Thameslink service but of the busy yards to which they gave access no trace remains.

**The Kent coalfield**
The east Kent coalfield was both small and relatively short lived. Even at its peak in the mid-1930s the four collieries produced only just over two million tons each year, 1% of the total British output and enough to supply only about 10% of the needs of south east England. Nevertheless, around 90% left the collieries by rail, making a significant contribution to revenue in a part of east Kent where freight traffic, apart from that to Dover, was not very heavy. The bulk of the output was used in Kent. In 1945 40% went to the paper and cement industries, 25% to power stations, 20% was used on the railways (mainly for top-link engines at Dover and Ramsgate) and the remainder went to gasworks or the London market.

Throughout the 19th century geologists argued over the existence of a coalfield in south east England, some suggesting that the deposits of South Wales and the Bristol region were continuous under the Thames Valley with those of the Pas de Calais in northern France. Proof that they were right came in 1890 when

boreholes put down by the Channel Tunnel Company at Dover located coal seams, with iron ore above, at a depth of 1,157ft. Further drilling over the next 20 years established the existence of a coalfield extending for around 250 square miles, some of it under the sea, in an area south of the Canterbury to Ramsgate line and east of the route from Canterbury to Dover.

Exploitation proved to be a difficult matter. Flooding, dangerous geological conditions and finance all created problems, for the pits were both deep and wet. One new mine was opened in each of the years between 1906 and the outbreak of World War 1, but several took a long time to become productive. There were numerous bankruptcies among the mining companies, the coalfield being frequently characterised as, literally, a bottomless pit as far as money was concerned. Several collieries did not survive and it was not until the 1920s that production became firmly established.

Of the four successful collieries, two, Snowdown and Chislet, were alongside main lines (Fig 8). Betteshanger, the last to open (in 1924) and the last to close was near the coastal route north of Deal and was at first served by a two-mile branch line and an extensive railway system. In later years only about half of

the branch survived, leading to a loading point for merry-go-round hopper wagons and linked to the colliery by a conveyor belt.

The provision of transport for the fourth colliery, Tilmanstone, provided the greatest railway interest. It was the only successful one of several opened up beneath the Chalk downland east and north of Shepherdswell and served by the East Kent Light Railway, promoted in 1910 by Kent Coal Concessions Ltd. and engineered by Colonel H.F Stephens. The railway was opened to Tilmanstone in 1912 and the colliery became productive in 1913; later, the railway was extended for several miles northwards towards Wingham and Sandwich. Although in terms of output Tilmanstone was the smallest of the Kent collieries, a steady flow of traffic took place for 70 years over the two and a quarter miles to Shepherdswell, although for a time in the 1930s an overhead ropeway took some of the output direct to Dover docks. Had the other three collieries it served been equally successful the light railway might more nearly have fulfilled the hopes of Colonel Stephens, although, because it did not provide a direct link to any major town, passenger traffic was doomed to failure. Nevertheless, with the utmost economy of operation, the railway maintained its independence until 1948.

After the cessation of passenger services in November 1948 and general freight traffic three years later the truncated remains of the East Kent Light Railway became the Tilmanstone Colliery branch of BR. It was served by up to nine return workings to and from Shepherdswell each day from Monday to Friday, most running in the morning and early afternoon. Because of its sharp curves the line was the exclusive haunt of the rebuilt Stirling 'O1' class, of which four were shedded at Dover mainly

**Some coal travelled to its destination as block loads such as this special passing Canterbury West on Thursday 2 April 1953 behind 'N' class No 31401. The SER station buildings, the signalbox spanning the tracks and semaphore signals still survive today, although the two through tracks have been taken out.** *Donald Kelk*

*Below:*
**A major component of freight traffic in Kent in the 1950s was fruit and vegetables in continental vans between Dover train ferry and the depots in south London. The 12.45pm Southwark to Dover train of empty vans is seen near Shepherdswell on Friday 13 August 1954 headed by 'King Arthur' No 30801** *Sir Meliot de Logres. R. A. King*

for this duty. They were the successors to similar engines which worked on the line in its independent days. Up to 26 wagons at a time were worked up and down the branch before being made up into larger loads for forwarding from Shepherdswell. The reign of the 'O1s', among the last pre-grouping engines to work in Kent, did not end until May 1960, when an '08'-type diesel shunter was tried. Although it encountered problems with slipping on the steep gradients, the replacement of the SECR veterans was by this time becoming imperative, and in due course the '08s' took over the duty. Not long before the line closed at the time of the 1984/5 coal strike (although official closure was not until 31 December 1987), Class 73 electro-diesels became the usual motive power following bridge strengthening near Tilmanstone.

On the main line regular coal trains ran between Sittingbourne and Shepherdswell and between Aylesford and Snowdown, with some of the output being collected by general goods trains which called at the colliery sidings. Up to seven freight trains a day from Deal or Dover called at Betteshanger *en route* for Ashford, Hoo or Minster, while the output of Chislet colliery was collected by trains which called on their way from Ashford to Minster, where there were extensive sidings used for marshalling coal trains.

By the early 1950s the area of Surrey around Waddon Marsh, on the West Croydon to Wimbledon line, had become a major centre for energy production, and block coal trains from Kent supplied both the gasworks and power stations. They travelled by way of north Kent and Bricklayers Arms or via the spur between Beckenham Junction and Norwood. Others went by way of Ashford, Tonbridge and Redhill, reversing in Norwood Yard. Later, in 1963, Richborough power station was opened in close proximity to the Kent coalfield to use its output as other markets, especially the railway, declined. But by then the postwar heyday of the coal industry was over as markets were lost to oil, then a very cheap fuel. Later, Richborough power station itself was converted to dual oil or coal firing.

Chislet colliery closed in late 1969 and, despite the existence of reserves totalling over 1,000 million tons, the remaining collieries closed within 20 years. Around 5,000 mining jobs disappeared and today the traveller through east Kent has to look hard to find evidence that a coal mining industry ever existed there.

*Left:*
**An everyday scene at Dover in 1953, with continental wagons being shunted off the train ferry by a 'C' class 0-6-0 No 31243. In the small hours of each morning the sleeping cars of the 'Night Ferry' passenger service were handled in the same way.**
*P. Ransome Wallis collection, National Railway Museum, York*

*Below:*
**A reminder of the importance of domestic vans traffic is provided by this view taken on 21 July 1951 of the 7.42pm train to Cannon Street leaving Ashford behind 'D1' No 1739. On the left is WD 2-8-0 No 90564, a type used in Kent for a short time after World War 2.** *J. J. Smith*

97

# Chapter 10

# Out of the ordinary

Coming at a time when they still had a dominant role in inland transport, the two world wars of the first half of the 20th century placed a great strain on Britain's railway companies. Nowhere was the pressure greater than on the SR, where large numbers of men and a vast amount of munitions had to be carried to the Channel ports and returning soldiers and prisoners of war moved inland on the first stage of the journey to camps and hospitals all over the country. To this had to be added the civilian traffic generated by moves such as the evacuation of children from London and other vulnerable areas like the Medway towns. It was as well that the operating department had at its disposal both a variety of routes between London and the Kent coast and the pool of engines and rolling stock used for the peacetime summer traffic, especially as the war inevitably brought losses of resources due to air raids and other enemy action.

The sheer number of special trains operated in the war years is mind boggling. According to Nock, (*The South Eastern and Chatham Railway*, p160), between 5 August 1914 and 31 December 1918 the SECR operated 101,872 specials, an average of 66 a day, excluding empties. Equally remarkable was the number of trains operated in connection with operation 'Dynamo', the evacuation of Dunkirk between 27 May and 4 June 1940.

Darwin (*War on the Line*, p24) records that in this period the SR operated 586 special trains from the Kent ports — 327 from Dover, 64 from Folkestone, 82 from Ramsgate, 96 from Margate and 17 from Sheerness, between them carrying 335,000 people. Nearly 2,000 coaches from each of the four railway companies were made up into 186 trains. Some of these made several journeys to and from the coast. The orderly supply of empty trains to prevent Dover from being overwhelmed was one of the major problems that had to be overcome.

The operation was all the more remarkable in that there was almost no opportunity to plan it in advance, everything being arranged on an *ad hoc* basis. In Darwin's words 'Even the men who drove the trains often didn't know where they were going. Sometimes they thought they did but the military authorities changed their mind about it while they were on their way. 'Stop

*Below:*
**A reminder of the wartime years when SR engines rendered redundant by the curtailment of local passenger services were sent on loan to other companies. Several 4-4-0s went to the LMS, including 'F1' No 1060, seen here in the Peak District at Buxton, carrying a '17A' (Derby) shedplate.** *L&GRP No 23889/Courtesy David & Charles*

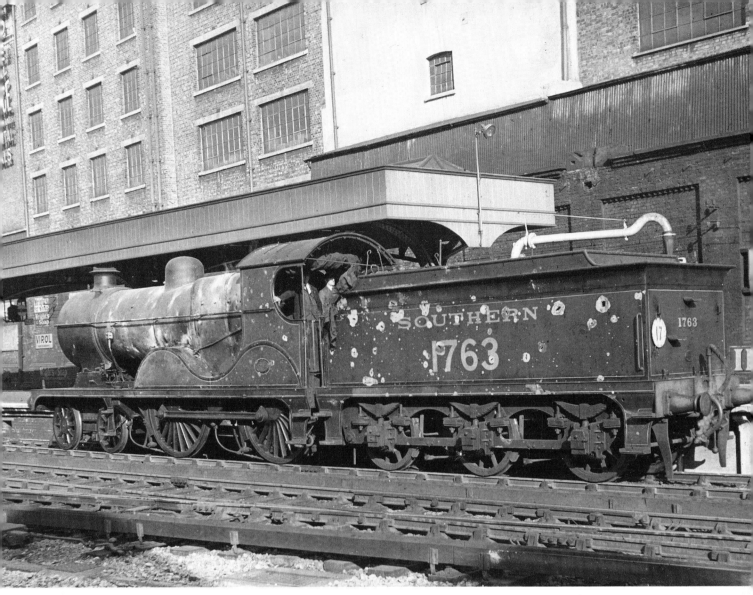

at Guildford and ask where you are going' was a typical instruction given, as were all others, by word of mouth. Yet the whole process went like clockwork. Train after train drew up; each was filled with tired and grimy men and, 20 minutes or so after its predecessor, rolled away into the blue, while another took its place'. Since the majority were heading for depots in the south and west of England, most went first to Tonbridge and then took the line to Redhill and thence to Guildford, Woking or Reading. At Redhill every train had to be reversed, requiring the provision of a newly serviced engine for the next stage of the journey. Problems like the disposal of a mountain of firebox ash and feeding the troops had to be dealt with. The latter was achieved by stopping trains at wayside stations like Headcorn, where 145,000 people

*Above:*
**This view of 'L' class 4-4-0 No 1763 at Victoria on 8 September 1940, damaged by enemy action, emphasises how much in the front line the railways of Kent were during World War 2. To be on the footplate of an engine subject to attack by gunfire must have been a horrific experience.** *By courtesy of the National Railway Museum, York*

*Below:*
**The great storm in early 1953 brought extensive flooding in north Kent, the main Thanet line being put out of action for five months. Damage was particularly severe on the section between Reculver and Birchington. Large quantities of chalk were brought into the area to help in the building of new sea walls and a trainload headed by a 'Q1' is seen being unloaded at Birchington.** *Revd A. W. V. Mace*

were fed during the operation. It was all a remarkable feat, for which the SR and its staff earned the deserved praise of a grateful nation.

After the war several legacies lingered on. In the late 1940s War Department 2-8-0s were to be seen on freight trains, while many specials for military personnel continued to operate, especially to the large camp at Shorncliffe. Forces traffic also brought other features of interest such as the special opening of the New Romney branch on Sunday evenings for an unadvertised train returning troops from weekend leave. Leaving Charing Cross at 9.20pm for Lydd Town, it usually consisted of a 'D' class pulling an SECR non-corridor 'long set'; the up working took place early on a Saturday afternoon to Cannon Street.

During 1953 two notable events occurred. Over the night of 31 January/1 February the combination of high tides and strong northerly winds associated with a deep depression over the North Sea drove a storm surge towards the Straits of Dover, causing extensive flooding along much of Britain's east coast south of the Humber and in the Low Countries. The north Kent marshes were severely affected, floodwaters covering thousands of acres to a considerable depth and washing away much of the track across the Swale marshes between Faversham and Whitstable and the marshes between Reculver and Birchington. Emergency services had to be instituted, bringing the reopening of several derelict or little used lines. Kent's oldest railway, the Canterbury and Whitstable, closed completely during the previous year, was used from 5 February for a few weeks to deliver coal to Whitstable, while first the Kearsney loop and then the

*Above left:*

**In the early days of the flood emergency, London to Ramsgate trains had to be take a very roundabout route from Faversham via Canterbury East, the Kearsney loop and Deal. The 12.20pm up train is seen entering the Kearsney loop on Saturday 14 February 1953 headed by 'Schools' No 30914** *Eastbourne.* **The line on the right is the direct route to Dover.** *S. C. Nash*

*Left:*

**The service on the section of the main line between Faversham and Herne Bay which remained operational was provided by push and pull trains. The 12.00 noon from Herne Bay is seen departing on Sunday 15 March 1953 with 'R' class No 31660 between the two sets of coaches.** *J. J. Smith*

*Below:*

**Drummond 'M7' class 0-4-4Ts, rare visitors to the Kent coast, also shared in working the emergency services. No 30052 is seen propelling out of Herne Bay. Its train includes a 'birdcage' brake, an unusual vehicle to find in an auto train.** *P. Ransome Wallis*

The second emergency to occur in 1953 came with the withdrawal of a number of Bulleid light Pacifics due to suspected axle defects. For a few weeks from mid May certain Thanet line trains were worked by 'B1' class 4-6-0s on loan to Stewarts Lane from former LNER sheds. This photograph features the 8.35am Victoria to Ramsgate train passing Herne Hill behind No 61329, lent by Stratford depot. *R. C. Riley*

*Below:*
In addition to the holiday and excursion trains, the Kent main lines saw other interesting workings. On Saturday 14 June 1958 the 4.25am Fishguard to Folkestone Harbour, carrying Irish pilgrims to Lourdes, was headed by 'S15' 4-6-0 No 30835, a type rarely seen in Kent after the 1930s. The engine was shedded at Redhill, mainly for use on Guildford line freight trains. *J. J. Smith*

Canterbury spur (Chapter 2) were reopened to enable trains from London to reach Thanet. The route via Kearsney was particularly roundabout, involving trains reaching Ramsgate via Canterbury East and Deal with stops at Kearsney and Martin Mill to attach and detach a pilot if the driver felt he needed one over the sharply curved one in 70 gradient between them. Use of this route lasted for only as long as it took to relay and reopen the Canterbury spur, this being done by 23 February.

Repairs to the line between Faversham and Whitstable were completed in time for a passenger service to resume running on 2 March, a shuttle being provided between Herne Bay and Faversham, where connection was made with Birchington-Ramsgate-London trains. Most of the shuttles were push and pull operated, consisting sometimes of two-car sets with the engine between, although this accommodation was quite insufficient for the number of commuters from the Herne Bay area. 'R' and 'H' class 0-4-4Ts were used at first but from mid-March Drummond LSWR 'M7' class 0-4-4Ts Nos 30052/3 and 30129, a type never popular at Kentish sheds, were sent to Faversham to work the Herne Bay shuttles.

Between Reculver and Birchington the floods made two breaches, 700 and 800yds long, in the sea wall. Two entirely new

walls had to be constructed jointly by BR and the Kent River Board, involving movement by rail of huge quantities of Chalk from Knockholt and a site near Ramsgate. A face 500ft long and 50-60ft high was made at Knockholt station to remove about 100,000 tons of rock. Up to eight trains a day, seven days a week, were worked via Chislehurst, Swanley and Chatham to Reculver, motive power ranging from 'King Arthurs' to 'N' class 2-6-0s and 'Q1s'. For working from the Ramsgate end 'Q1s' were also used. Work went on day and night, the line reopening for direct trains between London and Thanet on 21 May, just in time for the Whitsun holiday traffic.

Normal services had barely resumed when the Kent main lines were hit by a second crisis. This had its origin on the Waterloo to Exeter line when, on 24 April, 'Merchant Navy' No 35020 *Bibby Line* broke its driving axle at speed at Crewkerne, due to suspected metal fatigue. Luckily only the centre driving wheels derailed, but the decision was taken to withdraw all the 'Merchant Navies' for examination of the axles. This had little effect on the Kent lines apart from the appearance of two more 'Britannia' Pacifics Nos 70030/4 on loan from Longsight (Manchester) on boat train duties, including the Night Ferry. But when the light Pacifics were also checked and some defective axles were

*Right:*
**From time to time accidents occurred. Early in 1960 No 34084 *253 Squadron* ran through a sand drag at Hither Green while working a train of ferry wagons. This is the scene on Monday 29 February, with 'N' class No 31413 passing with an up freight. Hither Green was the site of a more serious accident a few years later involving the loss of life when a Hastings diesel multiple-unit derailed.** *R. C. Riley*

*Below right:*
**The scene at Victoria on 19 May 1957, with 'D1' No 31545 waiting to leave with the Stephenson Locomotive Society 'Chatham and Dover' special train. On the fastest postwar schedule to Margate, the train, driven by Sam Gingell, standing next to the smokebox, reached its destination in 85 minutes net.** *S. C. Nash*

*Below:*
**On Sunday 11 June 1961, the day before the start of full electric working on the Folkestone main line, 'L1' No 31786 piloted 'D1' No 31749 on the 'South Eastern Limited', seen near Teston Crossing Halt on the Maidstone West line. The train included two of the few surviving SECR ten compartment non-corridor coaches and a former Pullman car, by then painted in green livery.** *Mike Esau*

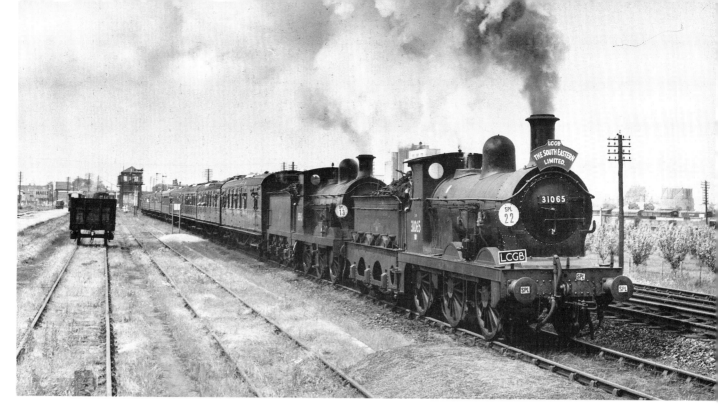

found a locomotive shortage loomed and, to make up the deficit, 15 ex-LNER 'B1' class 4-6-0s arrived on loan to Stewarts Lane. They came from far and wide:

Stratford (30A): 61109, 61329.
Norwich (32A): 61041, 61050.
New England (35A): 61138.
Colwick (38A): 61188, 61192.
York (50A): 61015, 61338.
Darlington (51A): 61273/4.
St Margaret's (Edinburgh) (64A): 61354.
Eastfield (Glasgow) (65A): 61133.
Carlisle Canal (68E): 61219.
Thornton Junction (62A): 61148.

While the 'B1s' worked mainly between Victoria and Ramsgate, they also saw service on the Central Section, notably on Newhaven Boat Trains. They commenced work on 20 May, No 61041 working the 8.35am from Victoria, while one was regularly employed on the 11.35am Victoria to Ramsgate, returning at 5.05pm. Under the care of Mr R. H. Hardy, himself an ex-Eastern Region man, the Stewarts Lane 'B1s' turned in some satisfactory performances, although the engine crews regarded them as

*Above:*

**The 'South Eastern Limited' leaving Paddock Wood for Hawkhurst headed by 'O1' No 31065 and 'C' No 31592. The 'O1' was withdrawn a few weeks later, but the 'C' continued for several more years as an Ashford Works shunter. It still survives on the Bluebell Railway.**
*P. J. Lynch*

rough and noisy compared with the resident Southern types.

However, the locomotive crisis was short lived and the Bulleid Pacifics were mostly back in service within a month, some 'B1s' only staying a few days at Stewarts Lane. By 20 June all except Nos 61015, 61273/4 and 61354 had been returned. By way of contrast the SR was able itself to help out three years later when the Western Region had temporarily to withdraw many of

*Below:*

**In freezing conditions on Sunday 25 February 1962, a 'King Arthur', No 30782 *Sir Brian*, returned to the South Eastern Division for the 'Kentish Venturer' tour. The engine is seen in a blizzard at Ashford shed along with 'Schools' No 30926 *Repton*, which also worked a section of the tour. Also dimly visible is a Sulzer Type 24 diesel, soon to leave the Southern Region on completion of delivery of the Type 33 Cromptons.** *Gerald Siviour*

*Above:*

**The 'Kentish Venturer' also made a journey to New Romney behind two surviving SECR veterans, 'H' class No 31263 and 'C' class No 31690. The pair are seen leaving Lydd Town. Passenger services on this branch lasted for a further five years with diesel traction, and this part still survives carrying a weekly nuclear flask train from Dungeness power station.** *Gerald Siviour*

its 'King' class, and Standard Class 5 4-6-0s from the SR went to join Stanier Pacifics on loan to the WR.

In the last days of steam in Kent a number of special trains were run for railway enthusiasts, usually offering a combination of a fast run behind one of the diminishing band of former main line engines and a tour of the remaining branch lines. In September 1954 two of the last unrebuilt and non-superheated Wainwright 4-4-0s Nos 31166 and 31737 bowed out in style with the RCTS 'Invicta Special', which they double headed from Ashford to Blackfriars on the final stage of a tour such as this. The pair distinguished themselves by hauling seven coaches from Ashford to Marden, 16.7 miles in just over 18 minutes, with a maximum speed of 70mph at Headcorn. In the following year the first closure of the Lewes to East Grinstead 'Bluebell' line was marked on 14 August by the running of another RCTS Special, the 'Wealden Limited', which travelled from Victoria via Swanley, Sevenoaks, Tonbridge, Hawkhurst and Hastings to reach Lewes before returning via East Grinstead to London. One of the tour highlights was the descent of Hildenborough bank, when 'E1' 4-4-0 No 31019, in charge of Driver Gingell, reached just over 84mph. The other highlight was the traversal of the 'Bluebell' line on a fine summer evening three months after its official closure to regular services behind Brighton 'Atlantic' No 32426 *St Alban's Head*.

Perhaps the finest performance came two years later, when 'D1' No 31545, again in charge of Sam Gingell, headed the

Stephenson Locomotive Society's 'Chatham and Dover' Special on 19 May. The train of six coaches (205 tons) was given the fastest schedule since 1939 from Victoria to Margate, being allowed 90 minutes for the 74 miles. Three downhill sprints of the type that made Sam Gingell and these engines famous (79mph at Farningham Road, 77mph down Sole Street bank and 80mph at Reculver) helped the train to reach Margate two minutes early in 85 minutes by the time allowance was made for permanent way slowings. Two rebuilt Stirling 'O1' class 0-6-0s Nos 31425 and 31434 then took the excursion on via the Kearnsey loop to Shepherdswell, Tilmanstone Colliery and Folkestone, reaching 50mph on the descent to Dover.

Electrification works in the subsequent years curtailed further attempts at high speed running on the Kent main lines but the Maunsell 4-4-0s were still around in the early 1960s to take part in the final steam excursions over the lines they had worked with distinction for over 40 years. For example, on 11 June 1961 'L1' No 31786 and 'D1' No 31749 headed a special which toured some SER lines on the last day of steam working. Later, 'O1' No 31065 and 'C' 31592 took the train to Hawkhurst and 'Terriers' Nos 32662 and 32670 worked from Robertsbridge to Tenterden on the day these two former Colonel Stephens lines were finally erased from the BR map.

The last fling for steam on the main lines came eight months later when, on 25 February 1962, a day of snow showers and a bitterly cold wind, one of the last 'King Arthur' class No 30782 *Sir Brian* worked round the coast from London to Margate and on to Ashford. The train was then taken down the New Romney branch before being returned to London by 'Schools' No 30926 *Repton*. To the authors a lasting memory of Kentish steam is of waiting to photograph this train, standing in a coal wagon to gain some protection from the biting north wind sweeping over Romney Marsh on that Sunday afternoon over 30 years ago.

# Chapter 11

# The decline and revival of steam

So far as the railways of Kent are concerned the British Transport Commission's railway modernisation plan announced early in 1955 largely confirmed what was thought to be Sir Herbert Walker's dream back in the 1930s — an all electric SR. Of the total of £1,240 million to be spent nationally over a period of 15 years, £185 million was to finance electrification, including most Southern lines east of a line from Reading to Portsmouth. This was to involve the conversion of some 250 route miles, a major exception being the Tonbridge to Hastings line, for which special diesel-electric units capable of working through the narrow tunnels were to be built. It was recognised that electrification would render redundant a large number of modern steam engines, particularly the Bullied Pacifics, and there was speculation that, following rebuilding, they might find employment elsewhere on BR.

An announcement soon followed that the first stage of the new electrification would be an extension of the third rail at 750V dc from Gillingham to Faversham (including the Sheerness branch) thence to Dover Marine and Ramsgate. Because of its heavy commuter traffic it was not surprising that this line was given precedence over the Folkestone route. Electrification would be accompanied by track quadrupling between Bickley and Swanley and between Rainham and Newington, partial doubling of the Sheerness line and the extension of colour light signalling from Brixton to Ramsgate. Station platforms would be lengthened to 810ft at most stations on the Ramsgate line and to eight coach lengths between Faversham and Dover. Some stations, for example St Mary Cray, Swanley and Newington would be rebuilt and new multiple unit depots provided. This work was to be completed by June 1959.

The second stage, to be completed by 1962, would involve electrification of 157 route miles extending from Sevenoaks to Dover and Folkestone Harbour, Maidstone East to Ashford and on to Ramsgate via Canterbury West, the coast route from Minster to Dover and the Paddock Wood to Maidstone West and the Hastings (Ore) to Ashford lines. The principal track works involved would be quadrupling between Saltwood and Folkestone and a third reversible track between Pluckley and Ashford.

Electrification was to bring about a quantum leap in service regularity and frequency. The main lines would have at least two trains an hour each way at regular times, one providing a stopping service and the other calling at principal stations. Wayside stations, previously served by notoriously infrequent and irregular trains (Chapter 8), would be provided with hourly services and some, for example on the Sheerness branch and between Maidstone East and Ashford, would have two trains to the hour. Canterbury would also gain by having two trains an hour on both routes to London although Maidstone, the county town, still had no fast services of its own. Some 220 new multiple-units would be required; originally 112 of them were to be four-car sets and the remainder two-car units, although in the event more four-car sets were provided. A number of motorised luggage vans were to be built for use on boat trains and parcel

*Above left:*
**The changing face of the Thanet line as it was being prepared for electrification in the late 1950s. This was the scene at St Mary Cray Junction on Saturday 22 September 1956, with 'King Arthur' No 30795 *Sir Dinadan* on an up express.** *R. C. Riley*

*Left:*
**The same location three years later. The tracks have been quadrupled and many features typical of the steam age railway, like semaphore signals and the pole line, have vanished. No 34066 *Spitfire* is seen heading an up Folkestone boat train on the last day of steam operation.** *R. C. Riley*

duties, while servicing facilities would include a new depot west of Ashford at Chart Leacon and extensive alterations at Ramsgate.

In order to eliminate steam working in Kent as quickly as possible orders were placed between 1957 and 1959 for 98 1,550hp diesel-electric locomotives with Sulzer engines and Crompton Parkinson electrical equipment to be built by the Birmingham Railway Carriage and Wagon Company. Intended mainly to be used on freight and vans trains, these highly reliable machines, later the Class 33, have seen extensive passenger duty all over the SR and beyond and without doubt were one of the most successful of the Modernisation Plan diesels. As a stop-gap until they were delivered, 16 boiler-fitted Sulzer Type 2s (later Class 24) were borrowed from the LMR and based at Hither Green, providing experience in diesel operation that proved invaluable when the Class 33 entered service.

The transition to an electrified and dieselised railway system took place more rapidly than the original scheme envisaged. Although problems were experienced while work progressed (Chapter 5), stage 1 was completed on time and over the weekend of 13-14 June 1959 the main line through Chatham saw its last official steam workings, although a few specials and boat trains were still steam powered until early in 1962. But the pressure was on to reduce and eliminate steam working as quickly as possible. The Crompton diesels began to enter service from Jan-

*Above right:*
**Quadrupling also took place between Rainham and Newington. In June 1958, when reliability and morale were at a low ebb, a grimy Standard Class 5 No 73085 is seen with an up express near Newington.**
*P. Ransome Wallis*

*Right:*
**In the months before electrification, crew training trips were run to prepare for the augmented services. 'H' class No 31266 is seen propelling an instruction saloon on a Gillingham to Ramsgate trip near Chestfield.** *P. Ransome Wallis*

*Below:*
**On Saturday 13 June 1959, the last weekend of steam on the Chatham line, 'U1' No 31907 takes Maunsell corridor coaches down to the Kent coast for the last time past Bickley, passing new electric units waiting to take over the service on Monday.** *R. C. Riley*

*Above:*
**Last night performance at Victoria on Sunday 14 June 1959. The final down steam hauled Ramsgate express at 8.35pm was hauled by the pioneer 'West Country' Pacific No 34001 *Exeter*, passing Ivatt 2-6-2T No 41291 on carriage pilot duties.** *Mike Esau*

*Left:*
**Victoria's last Kent coast steam train, the 8.52pm to Dover on 14 June 1959, was appropriately hauled by 'L1' No 31753, a class associated with this main line for over 30 years. A small wreath adorned the smokebox and a few people had gathered to witness the event, but nobody had bothered to clean the engine, a situation typical of the final dispirited years of Chatham line steam working.** *Mike Esau*

uary 1960; they were delivered at the rate of one per week and by the summer had taken over most of the Charing Cross to Dover and Ramsgate expresses, some of which were already being worked at weekends by Hastings line units. Steam still remained dominant, however, on boat trains.

Moves were also made to speed up progress with electrification with the aim of completion by 1961, a year earlier than anticipated. Priority was given to the lines in east Kent, as Ramsgate shed was in process of conversion to a multiple-unit depot. It closed to steam in December 1960 and the local services between Ramsgate and Dover went over to electric working on 2 January 1961. Five months later came a major step which brought about the elimination of main line steam in Kent when the line from Sevenoaks to Folkestone and Dover, along with the Paddock Wood to Maidstone West branch, was energised, although a new timetable was not introduced until the following year. Only the secondary route between Maidstone East, Ashford and Ramsgate continued to be worked as before, mainly with 2-6-4Ts, and these lines were also electrified with effect from October 1961.

The whole Kent coast electrification scheme was thus implemented in a little over two years, the only significant loss

*Above left:*
**In the aftermath of electrification some of the displaced steam engines went to the western and central divisions of the Southern Region. Among them were some 'L' and 'L1' class, sent to Nine Elms where they found limited use on vans trains and light passenger duties, but many, like 'L1' No 31789 seen here, spent most of their time in store. Some 'Schools' also went back to their prewar haunts, but fared little better and all were withdrawn by the end of 1962.** *Mike Esau*

*Left:*
**In 1960 it was decided to replace most of the remaining steam turns on the Folkestone line expresses with the newly available Crompton diesels, later to become Class 33. No D6549 is seen in May 1961 heading the 11.20am Ramsgate to Charing Cross through the Warren. The Class 33s were among the most successful diesels ordered in the 1950s and many are still at work 30 years later.** *M. Pope*

*Below:*
**Less successful than the Cromptons were the Class 24 Sulzers borrowed from the London Midland Region. Too underpowered for use singly on expresses, they spent much of their time either providing steam heating for trains hauled by the Cromptons, or on vans duties. One of them is seen emerging from Abbot's Cliff tunnel.** *Mike Esau*

*Right:*

**Also rather troublesome in their early days because of a tendency to excessive slipping were the Doncaster-built 2,550hp Bo-Bo electric locomotives (later Class 71). No E5014 is seen climbing Grosvenor bank on 12 March 1967 with the down 'Golden Arrow', which by then had only limited Pullman accommodation.**
*J. Scrace*

*Below right:*

**The lingering presence of steam at Ashford in early 1962. A few engines, including 'C' class No 31268, were maintained for humble but essential tasks like snowplough duties and works shunting, but the shed finally closed to steam in October 1963. The remaining steam shunters used at the works were then serviced there in a small shed.**
*Mike Esau*

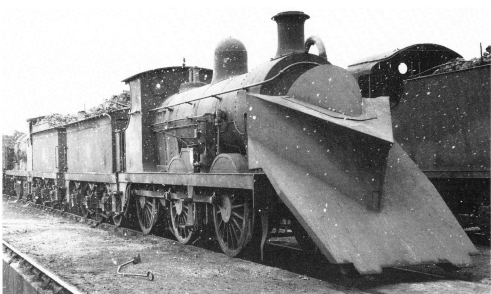

*Below:*

**After its closure for operating purposes, Ashford shed became for a while the 'South Eastern Steam Centre'. Among the engines based there at various times were 'O1' No 65 (the former No 31065) and 'H' class No 263 (formerly No 31263). The depot also housed three Pullman cars and the unique set of Bulleid double-deck coaches. Some of the stock is seen during a rare open day.** *John Everitt*

from the original plan being the failure to convert the Ashford to Hastings line, which still remains today an outpost of diesel electric multiple unit operation. By contrast the Tonbridge to Hastings line, not included in the original proposals, was electrified in the mid-1980s following track singling through its narrow tunnels. So far as one line, the Paddock Wood to Maidstone West route is concerned, electrification may well have been its salvation for it could have otherwise been a candidate for closure under the Beeching proposals published soon afterwards.

As with the spread of modernisation elsewhere there tended for a while to be odd survivors of steam operation. For example, as late as August 1961 the 5.45am London Bridge to Ashford via Hastings, returning from Ashford to Tonbridge as a stopping train, continued to be worked by a 'Schools' from Bricklayers Arms until the installation of colour light signals brought a ban on steam operation through Polhill and Sevenoaks tunnels, except in an emergency. Gradually the other survivors also faded

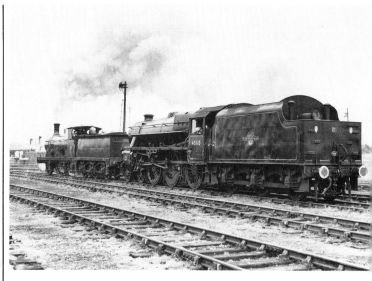

*Above right:*
**Other stock based at Ashford included 'C' class No 592 (formerly No 31592) and Stanier Class 5 No 45110, later named *Biggin Hill*, seen here on 29 March 1970. They subsequently went to the Bluebell Railway and the Severn Valley Railway respectively.** *S. C. Nash*

*Right:*
**For nearly 30 years until 1990, steam was absent from the main lines of Kent. Then, on 8 September, to mark the 50th anniversary of the Battle of Britain, No 34072, one of the former 'Night Ferry' engines shedded at Dover, returned to its old haunts to be renamed *257 Squadron*. The engine is seen at Folkestone Central, admired by young lads whose parents were probably only children when the sound of a Bulleid whistle last echoed over the roof tops of Folkestone.** *Mike Esau*

*Below:*
**Even better was to come in September 1991 when steam returned for two days to the Folkestone Harbour branch. 'West Country' Pacific No 34027 *Taw Valley* and 2-6-4T No 80080 made trips up and down the bank in glorious sunshine. The environment of the harbour station has changed a great deal since the days of the 'R1s' on the branch (Chapter 4). Only a week later came the news that regular ferry sailings to Boulogne were to end in December after nearly 150 years.** *Mike Esau*

away and there began the long absence of steam from the main lines in Kent that only finally ended in 1990.

As this book was written the same stagnation that characterised these lines in the last days of steam has affected the electric services, which await the arrival of the long-delayed new 'Networker' trains. Improvements like the provision of a weekday hourly fast service to Maidstone have been offset by deterioration elsewhere, such as the loss of refreshment facilities (other than mobile trolleys) and fast services to north Kent. The business trains to and from Cannon Street now take around 75 minutes to Whitstable, compared with 65 minutes in the early days of electrification and 70 minutes with steam. Fast services to Margate and Ramsgate, such as the 93 minute schedules to Margate of the early days of electrification, are also a thing of the past, partly because housing development along the line has made many more stops necessary. The improvements elsewhere in recent years and the generally poor state of the 30 year old rolling stock only serve to show how second rate the Kent coast services have become.

The future remains shrouded in uncertainty, particularly over whether the proposed high speed link between Cheriton and London will ever be built and what form it will take. In the immediate future the mid-1990s will see the coming of the 'Three Capitals' expresses between London and Paris or Brussels via the Channel Tunnel sharing the main line to London with the existing services, surely a recipe for chaos. After travelling over a purpose built high speed line to Calais and through the tunnel, the new trains will encounter the curves and speed restrictions of a line which originated from bits and pieces built in the 19th century and since tinkered with in an effort to bring it up to modern requirements. At night the old route between the coast and Redhill will have to carry the freight traffic bound for Willesden and beyond upon which rest hopes of diverting to rail some of the lorry traffic which now thunders through Kent. The inadequacy of the county's rail infrastructure for carrying the projected increase in traffic only serves to emphasise the contrast between the situation in Britain and that in the rest of Europe.

*Above left:*
**Events moved a stage further in 1992 when steam expresses were again seen on the SECR main line via Tonbridge. Shortly before midnight on Sunday 7 June, Class 4 4-6-0 No 75069, which began life as a Dover engine, has just drawn to a standstill at London Bridge alongside Pacific No 34027 *Taw Valley*, which had arrived shortly before with the 'Man of Kent' from Ashford.** *Mike Esau*

*Left:*
**A last memory of the early postwar heyday of Kentish main line steam. 'Battle of Britain' No S21C167 *Tangmere*, surrounded by the paraphernalia of the steam age, waits at Cannon Street with a train for the Chatham line, admired by train spotters of an earlier generation than those at Folkestone.** *Revd A. W. V. Mace*

# Appendix

Locomotives on shed at Ashford (74A), Tonbridge (74B) and at Ashford Works, on Tuesday 27 April 1954

## Ashford Works 1.30pm

| | | | | | |
|---|---|---|---|---|---|
| 'C' | 31576 | 31593 | 31720 | 31723 | |
| 'D' | s1493 | 31577 | | | |
| 'E' | 31315 | | | | |
| 'E4' | 32479 | 32559 | | | |
| 'E5' | 32588 | | | | |
| 'E6' | 32414 | | | | |
| 'H' | 31295 | 31319 | 31322 | 31522 | 31542 | 31544 |
| 'K' | 32340 | 32347 | | | |
| 'L' | 31768 | | | | |
| 'L1' | 31757 | | | | |
| 'N' | 31413 | 31841 | 31872 | 31873 | |
| 'Q1' | 33022 | 33027 | | | |
| 'R' | 31660 | | | | |
| 'R1' | 31010 (0-6-0T) | | | | |
| 'T9' | 30282 | | | | |
| 'U1' | 31890 | 31891 | 31895 | 31898 | 31904 | 31905 |
| 'W' | 31920 | 31925 | | | |

*Total 38*

## Ashford shed 2.30pm

| Class | No/Name | | | | |
|---|---|---|---|---|---|
| 'C' | 31219 | 31585 | 31589 | 31590 | 31694 | 31714 |
| | 31716 | | | | |
| 'D' | 31574 | | | | |
| 'E3' | 32170 | | | | |
| 'E4' | 32473 | 32487 | | | |
| 'H' | 31276 | 31500 | 31521 | 31543 | |
| 'L' | 31769 | 31771 | 31772 | 31774 | 31778 |
| 'N' | 31401 | 31402 | | | |
| 'N1' | 31879 | | | | |
| 'N15' | 30767 *Sir Valence* | | | | |
| | 30774 *Sir Geheris* | | | | |
| | 30801 *Sir Meliot de Logres* | | | | |
| | 30804 *Sir Cador of Cornwall* | | | | |
| 'O1' | 31048 | | | | |
| 'P' | 31325 | | | | |
| 'Q1' | 33035 | | | | |
| 'R1' | 31339 (0-6-0T) | | | | |
| 'U1' | 31896 | | | | |
| 'V' | 30939 *Leatherhead* | | | | |
| 'Z' | 30953 | | | | |
| LMR 2-6-4T | 42069 | 42077 | 42094 | 42097 | |

*Total 38*

## Tonbridge shed 5.15pm

| | | | | |
|---|---|---|---|---|
| 'C' | 31588 | 31717 | | |
| 'D1' | 31489 | 31727 | | |
| 'E' | 31166 | | | |
| 'E3' | 32454 | | | |
| 'E4' | 32503 | 32578 | 32580 | |
| 'H' | 31239 | 31261 | 31548 | |
| 'L' | 31761 | 31765 | | |
| 'N' | 31407 | 31862 | | |
| 'N15' | 30795 *Sir Dinadan* | | | |
| 'Q1' | 33029 | 33030 | 33032 | 33033 |
| 'R' | 31666 | | | |
| 'R1' | 31698 | 31704 (0-4-4T) | | |

*Total 24*

# Bibliography

Ashford Borough Council; *150 years of railway history;* Official programme; 1992.

Behrend G. and Buchanan G.; *Night Ferry;* Jersey Artists; 1985.

Bignall A.; *Hopping down in Kent;* Hale; 1977.

Body G.; *Railways of the Southern Region;* Patrick Stephens; 1984.

Darwin B.; *War on the line;* Reprinted by Middleton Press.

Hendy J.; *This is Dover and Folkestone;* Ian Allan; 1965.

Kidner R. W.; *The South Eastern Railway;* Oakwood Press; 1952.

Klapper C.; *Sir Herbert Walker's Southern Railway;* Ian Allan; 1973.

Mitchell V. and Smith K.; *Sittingbourne to Ramsgate;*
*Redhill to Ashford;*
*East Kent Light Railway;*
*Branch Line to Allhallows;*
*Ashford to Dover;*
*Dover to Ramsgate;* Middleton Press.

Nock O.S.; *The South Eastern and Chatham Railway;* Ian Allan; 1961.

Simmons J.; *The Railway in Town and Country, 1830-1914;* David and Charles; 1986.

Vaughan A.; *Obstruction Danger;* Guild Publishing; 1989.

White H. P.; *A Regional History of the Railways of Great Britain-Southern England;* David and Charles; 1969.

White H. P.; *Forgotten Railways: South East England;* David and Charles; 1987.

Winkworth D. W.; *Southern Titled Trains;* David and Charles; 1986.